## More Praise for Missional Renaissance

"Reggie hits it out of the park again! Few people have the intellectual acumen to understand, and the ability to communicate, the changing fusion of the Church and our culture like Reggie McNeal. This book incisively identifies the characteristics and implications of missional being that lead to missional ministry."
—Dr. Gregory A. Wiens, state
pastor of Florida, Church of God Ministries

"A changing world demands a changing church. Reggie McNeal's Missional Renaissance captures the essential elements of that change and gives pastors and church leaders a practical guide for re-imagining how the people of God are to engage in a redemptive task in our world."
—Kurt Fredrickson, director, Doctor of
Ministry Program, Fuller Theological Seminary

"There are a ton of 'how to' books offering techniques to shore up struggling congregations. Thankfully, this is not one of them. Instead, McNeal gets the real question right, and asks what it means if we allow our lives, our congregations, and our structures to be transformed by an uncompromised commitment to participate in God's mission in the world. As one committed to the institutional life of the church, I am profoundly grateful, and deeply moved, by Reggie McNeal's words."
—Rev. Wesley Granberg-Michaelson,
general secretary, Reformed Church in America

"Whether you use the word 'missional' in every other sentence or you're not even sure what it means, you should read this book. As the church heads into new waters, we could stand to have a few more maps. In this book Reggie McNeal, provides one for those wanting to enter the adventure."
—Greg Holder, lead pastor, Windsor Crossing,
Community Church, St. Louis, Missouri

# MISSIONAL
# RENAISSANCE

# MISSIONAL RENAISSANCE

## Changing the Scorecard for the Church

Reggie McNeal

A LEADERSHIP NETWORK PUBLICATION

JOSSEY-BASS
A Wiley Imprint
www.josseybass.com

Published by Jossey-Bass
A Wiley Imprint
989 Market Street, San Francisco, CA 94103-1741—www.josseybass.com

**Library of Congress Cataloging-in-Publication Data**
McNeal, Reggie.
    Missional renaissance : changing the scorecard for the church/Reggie McNeal.—1st ed.
        p.   cm.
    Includes bibliographical references and index.
    ISBN 978-0-470-24344-2 (cloth)
    1. Mission of the church.   2. Church renewal.   3. Christianity—Forecasting.   I. Title.
    BV601.8.M395   2009
    266—dc22

                                                            2008041916

Printed in the United States of America
FIRST EDITION
*HB Printing*            10  9  8  7  6  5  4  3  2  1

# LEADERSHIP NETWORK TITLES

*The Blogging Church: Sharing the Story of Your Church Through Blogs*, Brian Bailey and Terry Storch

*Leading from the Second Chair: Serving Your Church, Fulfilling Your Role, and Realizing Your Dreams*, Mike Bonem and Roger Patterson

*The Way of Jesus: A Journey of Freedom for Pilgrims and Wanderers*, Jonathan S. Campbell with Jennifer Campbell

*Leading the Team-Based Church: How Pastors and Church Staffs Can Grow Together into a Powerful Fellowship of Leaders*, George Cladis

*Organic Church: Growing Faith Where Life Happens*, Neil Cole

*Off-Road Disciplines: Spiritual Adventures of Missional Leaders*, Earl Creps

*Reverse Mentoring: How Young Leaders Can Transform the Church and Why We Should Let Them*, Earl Creps

*Building a Healthy Multi-Ethnic Church: Mandate, Commitments, and Practices of a Diverse Congregation*, Mark DeYmaz

*Leading Congregational Change Workbook*, James H. Furr, Mike Bonem, and Jim Herrington

*The Tangible Kingdom: Creating Incarnational Community*, Hugh Halter and Matt Smay

*Leading Congregational Change: A Practical Guide for the Transformational Journey*, Jim Herrington, Mike Bonem, and James H. Furr

*The Leader's Journey: Accepting the Call to Personal and Congregational Transformation*, Jim Herrington, Robert Creech, and Trisha Taylor

*Whole Church: Leading from Fragmentation to Engagement*, Mel Lawrenz

*Culture Shift: Transforming Your Church from the Inside Out*, Robert Lewis and Wayne Cordeiro, with Warren Bird

*Church Unique: How Missional Leaders Cast Vision, Capture Culture, and Create Movement*, Will Mancini

*A New Kind of Christian: A Tale of Two Friends on a Spiritual Journey*, Brian D. McLaren

*The Story We Find Ourselves In: Further Adventures of a New Kind of Christian*, Brian D. McLaren

*Missional Renaissance: Changing the Scorecard for the Church*, Reggie McNeal

*Practicing Greatness: 7 Disciplines of Extraordinary Spiritual Leaders*, Reggie McNeal

*The Present Future: Six Tough Questions for the Church*, Reggie McNeal

*A Work of Heart: Understanding How God Shapes Spiritual Leaders*, Reggie McNeal

*The Millennium Matrix: Reclaiming the Past, Reframing the Future of the Church*, M. Rex Miller

*Shaped by God's Heart: The Passion and Practices of Missional Churches*, Milfred Minatrea

*The Missional Leader: Equipping Your Church to Reach a Changing World*, Alan J. Roxburgh and Fred Romanuk

*The Ascent of a Leader: How Ordinary Relationships Develop Extraordinary Character and Influence*, Bill Thrall, Bruce McNicol, and Ken McElrath

*Beyond Megachurch Myths: What We Can Learn from America's Largest Churches*, Scott Thumma and Dave Travis

*The Elephant in the Boardroom: Speaking the Unspoken About Pastoral Transitions*, Carolyn Weese and J. Russell Crabtree

# CONTENTS

About Leadership Network    xi

Introduction    xiii

**1**    The Missional Renaissance    1

**2**    Missional Manifesto    19

**3**    Missional Shift 1: From an Internal to an
        External Focus    41

**4**    Changing the Scorecard from Internal to
        External Focus    67

**5**    Missional Shift 2: From Program Development
        to People Development    89

**6**    Changing the Scorecard from Measuring
        Programs to Helping People Grow    111

**7**    Missional Shift 3: From Church-Based to
        Kingdom-Based Leadership    129

**8**    Changing the Scorecard from Church-Based to
        Kingdom-Based Leadership    157

Conclusion    177

Notes    183

The Author    187

Index    189

*To Wally Hawley, missional champion*

# About Leadership Network

Since 1984, Leadership Network has fostered church innovation and growth by diligently pursuing its far-reaching mission statement: to identify, connect, and help high-capacity Christian leaders multiply their impact.

Although Leadership Network's techniques adapt and change as the church faces new opportunities and challenges, the organization's work follows a consistent and proven pattern: Leadership Network brings together entrepreneurial leaders who are focused on similar ministry initiatives. The ensuing collaboration—often across denominational lines—creates a strong base from which individual leaders can better analyze and refine their own strategies. Peer-to-peer interaction, dialogue, and sharing inevitably accelerate participants' innovation and ideas. Leadership Network further enhances this process through developing and distributing highly targeted ministry tools and resources, including audio and video programs, special reports, e-publications, and online downloads.

With Leadership Network's assistance, today's Christian leaders are energized, equipped, inspired, and better able to multiply their own dynamic kingdom-building initiatives.

Launched in 1996 in conjunction with Jossey-Bass (a Wiley imprint), Leadership Network Publications present thoroughly

researched and innovative concepts from leading thinkers, practitioners, and pioneering churches. The series collectively draws
from a range of disciplines, with individual titles offering perspective on one or more of five primary areas:

1. Enabling effective leadership
2. Encouraging life-changing service
3. Building authentic community
4. Creating kingdom-centered impact
5. Engaging cultural and demographic realities

For additional information on the mission or activities of
Leadership Network, please contact:
Leadership Network
(800) 765-5323
client.care@leadnet.org

# INTRODUCTION

When it comes to being missional, it seems everyone wants in on the action. Do a Google search on "missional," and you will get well over a million hits, the number growing every minute. Publishers want "missional" in their book titles. Church Web sites tout their missional orientation. Denominations hold conferences on helping their constituents become more missional. Even some seminaries claim they are going missional.

So what's the big deal about being missional? And why does everybody seem to be staking out a missional claim?

The rise of the missional church is the single biggest development in Christianity since the Reformation. The post-Reformation church of the modern era differed remarkably from its medieval predecessor. The missional church will just as dramatically distinguish itself from what we now call "church."

Whereas the Reformation gifted us with a plethora of denominations distinguished by doctrine and polity, the missional movement actually simplifies the taxonomy of Christianity into two groups: those who get it and those who don't. And as a friend of mine likes to say, "If you have to ask what 'it' is, you don't get it." The ones who get it (the missional thing) come from every tribe in the universe of Christianity. They have more in common with others who get it, no matter what tribe or tradition they are from, than they have in common with those in their own tribe who don't get it. The missional din is the result of their calling out to one another, to locate others of their persuasion so they can link together and forge a new expression of life.

*Missional is a way of living, not an affiliation or activity.* Its emergence springs from a belief that God is changing his conversation with the world and with the church. Being missional involves an active engagement with this new conversation to the point that it guides every aspect of the life of the missional believer. To think and to live missionally means seeing all life as a way to be engaged with the mission of God in the world.

This missional understanding of Christianity is undoing Christianity as a religion. The expression of the Christian movement in North America is fundamentally altering before our very eyes. The shifts are tectonic. They involve both form and content. These developments go way beyond denominational affiliations, party labels (liberal, conservative, mainline, evangelical), corporate worship styles (contemporary, traditional), program methodological approaches (purpose-driven, seeker-friendly), or even cultural stances (postmodern, emergent, emerging). The missional development goes to the very heart of what the church is, not just what it does. It redefines the church's role in the world in a way that breaks sharply with prevailing church notions. These differences are so huge as to make missional and nonmissional expressions of Christianity practically unrecognizable to each other.

While much has been made of the deconstructive nature of missional Christianity, this aspect of the movement needs to be seen for what it is. In the early stages of movements, proponents have to distinguish the new from the status quo. What it *is not* is as important as what it *is*. However, as the movement matures, what it *is* becomes more fully defined and capable of supporting its own existence without having to live off siphoned energy or allergic reactions to the prior thing-it-is-not. Actually, movements that cannot get to this stage don't survive; they last only as long as the reactionary core can generate enthusiasm among the initial adherents and the disgruntled they recruit. In early stages of movements, the new thing and thing-it-is-not often alternately seek mutual ground and work to make the other go away.

We are still in the early days of the missional movement. Although it has been on the screen of radicals and revolutionaries for some decades, it has just recently broken into mainstream attention in the church. This means that for now, the discussion of what being missional is must still include how it is distinguished from what it is not. What it is not is church-as-usual. Early and previous writers in the missional movement (including me) have rehearsed the failures of the church and have given voice to the frustration of those who yearn for more than they are experiencing in their current church life. Various levels of deconstruction have been necessary to help people see that something different is possible.

It seems to me that we have now reached a tipping point in the missional movement. I say this because the questions I field from church leaders have changed. When I released *The Present Future: Six Tough Questions for the Church* (Jossey-Bass, 2002), I encountered a number of people asking me why I wrote what I did. Then my correspondence shifted to "This is how I feel; I just didn't know how to say it." Now the question I hear most often is "How can we do this?" This remarkable transition has taken place in a few short years. The tone of those posing the current questions reflects a hopeful determinism to become part of what God is up to.

I think we are in a kind of missional renaissance, where the confluence of thinking by key thinkers is reshaping the landscape of our imagination of what we think the church can and should be. One benefit of this missional renaissance is that we can now begin to say what missional is, not just what it is not. This ability in itself will accelerate the movement. The result will be that within a few years, it will be impossible to think of church the way we used to, as something we "went to" or "participated in" or "joined" or "attended."

I have witnessed numerous conversions to missional over the past decade. By observing and helping leaders commence the missional journey over and over again, I have come to realize some key transitions or shifts that must be negotiated in moving from institutional church experience into a missional expression of life and faith. This volume attempts to spell out just what these fundamental shifts are. The shifts are explained in the early pages of this book and are explored throughout in term of their implications. As leaders adopt these shifts, the missional renaissance will gain momentum.

Going missional will require that you make three shifts, both in your thinking and in your behavior:

- From internal to external in terms of ministry focus
- From program development to people development in terms of core activity
- From church-based to kingdom-based in terms of leadership agenda

These shifts are the signature characteristics of what missional means. They are not destinations; they are compass settings. They point you into the new world. They will move you from doing church as primarily a refuge, conservator, and institutional activity in a post-Christendom culture to being a risky, missionary, organic force in the increasingly pre-Christian world in North America.

I have shared these three shifts with thousands of church leaders across the country. Consistently I have seen these leaders respond with enthusiasm and hope. Their enthusiasm rises because these shifts express their inner convictions, giving voice to what it is they really want to do. These leaders gain hope because these shifts give them a way forward. Spiritual leaders in places of responsibility need more than deconstruction.

They know the jig is up, but they have Sunday coming and want to know how to recalibrate their efforts and ministries to be more missional.

These three shifts call for a new scorecard for the missional church. The typical church scorecard (how many, how often, how much) doesn't mesh with a missional view of what the church should be monitoring in light of its mission in the world. The current scorecard rewards church activity and can be filled in without any reference to the church's impact beyond itself. Since it is a fundamental truism of human nature that "what gets rewarded gets done," it is completely understandable that the current scorecard promotes the internally focused, program-based, church-based side of the ledger. We must develop a score-card that supports the other side of the shifts: externally focused ministry, people development efforts, and a kingdom-oriented leadership agenda. This new scorecard, more dimensional than our current one, will highlight new behaviors that will support and accelerate the rise of the missional church in North America.

My intended audience for this book includes those who exercise spiritual leadership in whatever capacity, especially if it involves your desire to lead others into the missional experience. I am writing also for the thousands of people who are part of ministry or church organizations who feel convinced that there has to be something better than they are experiencing. My hope is that you, no matter your scope of influence, will become missional viral agents in the environments where you serve and where you live out your faith. I believe we are already seeing signs of a missional pandemic.

We are privileged to be alive at a critical juncture in the history of the Christian movement in North America. The choices you and others make will influence the expression of the church for generations to come. Many will choose to hunker down and wait for the storm to blow over. It won't.

The original Renaissance paved the way for the Reformation, provoking a crisis in the church. The same thing is happening today. Just as in those days, you will have to choose sides. I am writing for those who are ready to declare they will go with what God is doing.

This is your invitation to join the missional renaissance.

# MISSIONAL
# RENAISSANCE

# 1

# THE MISSIONAL RENAISSANCE

The missional renaissance is under way. Signs of it are everywhere. Churches are doing some "unchurchy" things. A church in East Texas decides that its next ministry chapter should be about building a better community, not building a better church. "No child will go hungry in this county," the pastor declares in his "vision" message, a time usually reserved for launching new church initiatives. A church in Ohio passes up the option to purchase a prime piece of real estate that would allow it to build a facility to house its multisite congregation. Instead, it votes not to spend $50 million on church facilities but to invest the money in community projects. A congregation located in a town housing a major correctional facility has taken on the challenge of placing every released inmate in some kind of mentorship and sponsorship upon leaving prison. These efforts are resulting not just in cooperation from the prison but in a drop in recidivism rates as well. Another group of churches is collaborating on bringing drinkable water to villages in the developing and undeveloped nations of the world.

New expressions of church are emerging. One pastor has left a tall-steepled church to organize a simple neighborhood gathering of spiritual pilgrims. He is working at secular employment so that he doesn't have to collect monies to support a salary; rather, he and his colleagues are investing in people on their own street. A church planter who left an established church to start one of his own has decided to set up a network of missional communities to serve as the organic church in every sector of his city. Another entrepreneurial spiritual leader has opened up a community center with a church tucked inside of it. He has a dozen other ministries operating in the shared space.

The impact of the missional renaissance extends beyond the church into the social sector. The head of a homeless shelter in the Deep South has shifted his strategy from a food-and-counseling model to a coaching-and-employment model. Rather than relying on the "mouths fed and beds occupied" scorecard, he is insisting on new metrics to measure the life progress of the people he serves. His staff of "life coaches" are throwing themselves into people development, not just delivery of a ministry service.

Individual Jesus followers are also increasingly unwilling to limit their spiritual lives to church involvement. They are arranging their lives around their convictions and taking to the streets. A young husband and wife decide to live in a low-income apartment so they can serve as community developers for the complex. The complex owner does not mind that they are followers of Jesus or that they hold Bible studies and prayer meetings along with their pool parties and life skills workshops. A local businessman retires and calls on all his former business connections to contribute to a construction ministry he starts to help poor people fix up their homes.

The missional renaissance is changing the way the people of God think about God and the world, about what God is up to in the world and what part the people of God play in it. We are learning to see things differently, and once we adjust our way of seeing, we will never be able to look at these things the way we used to.

A similar dynamic has happened before. During the 1400s, the most gifted and passionate artists, writers, architects, and mathematicians of the day converged in Florence,

Italy, and other cities across Europe. With the sponsorship of the Medicis and other wealthy patrons, their cross-pollination of ideas and practices gave rise to the Renaissance. Their fertilized thought was both disruptive and creative. Old ways and beliefs were abandoned, forsaken for something better, something promising, something hopeful.

Once the Renaissance was begun, there was no going back. The trajectories of literature, religion, art, science, and even economics and political theory would all be altered by Renaissance thinking. A Ptolemaic view of the universe yielded to a new Copernican reality. The application of mathematics to drawing resulted in the development of perspective in art. Real-life representations in paintings replaced medieval iconic figures. It would be impossible for people to think about things post-Renaissance the same way they thought pre-Renaissance. Every part of culture was changed, including the church.

Similar forces are driving today's missional renaissance. Elevated educational levels, heightened technology, and increased wealth have combined to create a huge pool of talented activists and sponsors. A growing number of people are willing and able to engage social issues with new solutions and the power to make a difference. The combination of wealth, talent, and creativity is resulting in ideas and practices that are both disruptive and hopeful for the church. New ways of being church are being born every day. There is no putting this Humpty Dumpty back together. That's the good news. Church will never be the same.

The missional church renaissance is not occurring in a vacuum. Just as in the fifteenth century, larger social forces are at work that conspire to create conditions ripe for this kind of development. The confluence of three significant cultural phenomena is fueling the current collaboration and creativity:

- The emergence of the altruism economy
- The search for personal growth
- The hunger for spiritual vitality

These three elements anticipate the three shifts that people and churches must make to engage the missional renaissance. They serve as a starting point in our exploration of the missional church and how you can get in on it.

## Emergence of the Altruism Economy

Wealthy patrons bankrolled the initial Renaissance. The altruism economy is sponsoring this one.

The March 9, 2008, edition of the *New York Times Magazine* was titled "Giving It Away." Various articles chronicled the evolution of altruism, celebrity chefs' cooking for charity, four stories of individual twenty-somethings' efforts to change their piece of the world, and an interview with Dr. Larry Brilliant, head of corporate giving at Google. The thread that ran throughout the magazine is that we are witnessing something truly phenomenal in both the magnitude and the creativity of people's determination not just to share their wealth but to make a difference with it. The *Times* edition came a few months after the release of Bill Clinton's *Giving*[1] and hit the stands during the *Oprah's Big Give* television series. Celebrities like Bill and Melinda Gates, Warren Buffett, Bono, and Angelina Jolie target disease, Third World debt, illiteracy, and other social ills on a global scale.

But we also discover in every community nameless heroes who volunteer in soup kitchens, tutor struggling kids in English and math, build houses for people who can't afford them, and perform innumerable acts of kindness and generosity. And they give money—a lot of money. Charitable giving now comes to around $300 billion a year and is rising.

Altruism shows up in every sector of the economy. Every major corporation, and most minor ones, assign their managers community service obligations. A growing number of businesses dedicate a certain percentage of sales to performing altruistic work, from digging wells to provide safe drinking water overseas to supporting local school projects. Special Web sites are donated to organizations, allowing people not just to direct their own money but also to release others' resources for projects of their choice. FreeRice.com is an example of this development, with up to half a million people participating daily, freeing 400 metric tons of rice for hunger relief. Family foundations support favorite causes and local giving circles fund the arts in their communities. Hospitals provide millions of dollars in free services each year. Schools and student organizations unleash tens of thousands of volunteer hours into their communities through their campus service projects. The entertainment industry throws money at charity benefits. *American Idol* raised millions in one night, and *Extreme Makeover: Home Edition* has inspired hundreds of copycat local renditions.

The emergence of the altruism economy signals the positive inclination of people to believe that they can and should make a difference, starting with their neighborhood and extending to the entire globe. They also expect the people they deal with in commerce, the schools they attend, the businesses they support—and the churches they belong to—to be investing in making the world a better place.

This increased spirit of altruism is calling the church out to play. It beckons the church to move from being the recipient of a generous culture (religious causes garner the largest percentage of charitable dollars—about a third) to actually being generous to the culture. It challenges the church to move beyond its own programs and self-preoccupation. And it promises that once the church ventures into the street to engage human need, it will have many partners from all domains of culture to join with it in creating a better world.

This explosion of good actually creates a chance for the church to gain relevance and influence. But only if the church is willing to get out of the church business and get over the delusion that the "success" of the church impresses the world. It does not. It only impresses church people, while making others even more skeptical of the church's true motives. After chronicling the negative image of Christianity among younger generations in their groundbreaking book *Unchristian*, David Kinnaman and Gabe Lyons conclude, "No strategy, tactics, or clever marketing campaign could ever clear away the smokescreen that surrounds Christianity in today's culture. The perception of outsiders will change only when Christians strive to represent the heart of God in every relationship and situation."[2]

The way forward for churches that want to redefine their position in the community will be through service and sacrifice. In classic Renaissance dynamics, this approach is rediscovering and reapplying an ancient idea. The early church movement was characterized by this posture of service. Recapturing that character will require the church to make a major shift into a kingdom way of thinking and seeing. This shift will show up in a new scorecard highlighting different factors and behaviors than the ones that are typically tracked (attendance, monies received, activities at church). These new metrics will push beyond the church's own internal measures to monitoring the church's positive community impact beyond its walls.

## Missional Shift 1: From an Internal to an External Ministry Focus

The church must shift from an internal to an external focus in its ministry. This reflects what missional churches and missional church leaders are doing and why they are doing it. They don't focus beyond the church to be culturally hip. They make this shift because the new direction defines who they are. The missional church engages the community beyond its walls because it believes that is why the church exists.

This shift redefines the target of ministry. Internally focused churches and ministries (and people, for that matter) consume most of their energy, time, and money on a wide range of concerns, from survival to entertainment. Success in the internally focused culture is defined in terms of organizational goals. Leaders in these situations focus their efforts on helping the ministry achieve these goals (attendance, budget, new program widgets, improved widget performance). In other words, the scorecard is tied to activity focused on the organization itself.

Externally focused ministry leaders take their cues from the environment around them in terms of needs and opportunities. They look for ways to bless and to serve the communities where they are located. Much of their calendar space, financial resources, and organizational energy is spent on people who are not a part of their organization. These ministry ventures may or may not improve the organization's bottom line in terms of traditional measures (attendance may actually go down if people are released to mission). These leaders increasingly look to network with other leaders and organizations with similar passions in order to synergize their efforts and increase the impact of their ministry efforts.

Shifting from an internal to an external focus usually requires a radical change of mind-set on the part of the leader, away from being ruled by the constraints and scorecards of the internally focused system. Many leaders have spent their entire leadership lives in pursuit of building great organizations that rise to the top of church industry standards. Changing values and motivations is not easy, but nothing less will accomplish this shift. Not to mention the fact that leaders generally know how to "do church" (even if it is a guaranteed losing season), but they don't know if they have the requisite competencies to do anything else. After all, their training, roles, and status are tied to their church culture performances, not to their community awareness and contributions.

## The Search for Personal Growth

It is no accident that people pulled millions of copies of Rick Warren's *Purpose-Driven Life* off the shelf. They want to grow, and they want their lives to matter. Just check out the self-improvement section of your local bookstore. It dwarfs many other areas. Or take a look at what colleges and universities are offering, and filling up, in terms of adult education opportunities—everything from second-career (or third!) preparation to the advanced pursuit of leisure hobbies and interests. Check out the cable TV listings of shows offering advice to help people decorate, cook, dress, garden, manage money, train a dog, or flip a house. Life coaching has become a major industry. Many therapists are moving from traditional pathology-based approaches to more holistic, interventionist, proactive coaching, recognizing that people are searching for life change and development.

This unprecedented pursuit of personal development can be traced to several key changes. In the second half of the twentieth century, wave after wave of technology pushed people to adopt the mentality that they would need to engage in lifelong learning. Thanks to the Web and wireless access, information is now ubiquitous and asynchronous. Need to know something? Google it! You can suck the entire Library of Congress out of thin air! Right now!

Paradoxically, the more knowledge is available to us, the more we feel we need to learn. Far from satisfying our curiosity to know stuff, the onslaught of information fuels it. So a pervasive sense of needing to grow, to learn, to adapt, and to change has taken residence in the psyche of people in our culture.

The availability of information also does something else. It empowers people. Consider just one example—education. In a previous world, now made ancient by the digital revolution, people used to have to go to certain places and to certain people to acquire the knowledge necessary for an education. The educational system was built around an information acquisition and transfer modality, involving a largely didactic process from teacher to student. In this system, the learned instructor, the one with the information, passed knowledge down to the supplicant learner during certain hours of the day on certain days of the week in certain months of the year. We even built buildings where this knowledge transfer could occur, sending out buses to gather the learners. It was mass standardized education.

Forget that! Today, people learn at their own speed, on their own time, at their own convenience. In this new arrangement, power is ultimately transferred to the information consumer. Learners get to craft their own learning path.

The availability of information has increased empowerment. People are empowered to do for themselves things they once had to rely on others to do—others with the information and connections—like ticket agents who alone had seating charts for airplanes or stock brokers who alone had access to the stock market or any of hundreds of other examples. Some of you have never known a world where you had to wait for the bank to open and then ask someone there to manage your accounts. People like the idea of being able to manage the transactions of their lives. More than that, they expect it! They also want to and expect to be able to maximize their own personal development—whether at work or in their hobbies or recreational pursuits.

Not only do people want to grow themselves, but they also want to make sure other people have the same option. They want to invest in people, to lift the life experience of people less fortunate. To make these investments, people are now capable of and inclined toward researching problems and funding their ideas of solutions. And they are also increasingly determined to make sure their social capital is used efficiently and effectively to produce the results in people's lives they seek to achieve. Nearly gone are the days when charities could ask donors for money based just on how much activity the charitable organizations generate. Donors want impact—in people terms.

When you combine this commitment to personal development with the rise of the altruism economy, you arrive at the missional renaissance.

## Missional Shift 2: From Program Development to People Development

The confluence of these two cultural trends calls for the second shift of the missional church: from a focus on programs to a focus on people and their development as the core activity of the community of faith. If we only make the first shift without understanding and implementing this one, we wind up replacing an old program (church stuff) with a new program (community service) or another set of activities layered on top of what is currently being done. People will be worn out, maybe even at an accelerated pace—the very opposite result of what needs to happen.

Program-driven churches and ministry organizations operate on suspect but often unchallenged assumptions. These assumptions are that people will be better off if they just participate in certain activities and processes that the church or organization has sanctioned for its ministry agenda. The problem is that study after study continues to reveal that active church members do not reflect a different value set than the culture at large. In addition, they are beset by the same lifestyle ills of nonparticipants. They wonder, "Where's the abundant life that was promised if we only participated more?" The answer is that achieving abundant life will require intentional personal development. This is not a given in the program-driven modality of operation; the only *real* guarantee is that the church will keep people busy.

The missional church takes far more seriously the challenge to help people shape their path for personal development. Some of the key ideas we will explore for making this shift will challenge prevailing notions of how people grow that have shaped much of the program-driven church. We must change our ideas of what it means to develop a disciple, shifting the emphasis from studying Jesus and all things spiritual in an environment protected from the world to following Jesus into the world to join him in his redemptive mission. We need to expand the bandwidth of issues we address in helping people grow, realizing that there is no such thing as spiritual growth apart from relationship health and other life factors.

This shift is the most difficult of the three shifts necessary for going missional. This is true for several reasons. First of all, helping people grow and develop is hard work; it isn't something you start and finish in a twelve-week course. Second, the shift from pursuing institutional goals and objectives to measuring the impact of ministry on people's quality of life calls for a dramatically new scorecard. In the program-driven modality, the assumption was that if the church was doing well at providing and executing programs, people who participated in them automatically experienced personal growth. This assumption is no longer valid, and perhaps it never was.

Another reason this shift will prove difficult is that church leaders are not prepared for a life of people development. Typical clergy training efforts, including Bible colleges, seminaries, and denominational and parachurch ministries, prepare church leaders to teach the Bible, manage the church, and grow the business. The typical clergyperson is groomed to do project management (yes, even the sermon is a project) and perform religious rites, not develop people. And if the truth be known, many leaders do not give themselves to developing other people because they have never had it happen to them. Leaders will have to travel a steep unlearning curve to move away from the activities and behaviors that support the program-driven model.

This shift also means that church membership or some level of involvement in a local congregation will no longer be the primary spiritual expression of missional followers of Jesus. Missional Christians will no longer be content to help their church succeed in getting better at "doing church" or consider their commitment to the church as an expression of their spiritual depth. They are shifting their commitments to people and causes beyond the church. They also no longer look to or rely on the clergy and church leaders to script or dictate their spiritual and personal development. The church has to recalibrate its ministry efforts to champion this new reality.

The missional church provides an alternative to a failed system. No one can legitimately claim that our current model produces vibrant disciples. North American church attendees lack the caliber and character of disciples that we see in many other parts of the world where the movement started by Jesus is exploding, where the focus is on developing people, not just processing them.

## The Hunger for Spiritual Vitality

The quest for spirituality as a central tenet of postmodern life has been amply chronicled by scores of researchers and cultural analysts. This development reverses a centuries-old trend set in motion by the fifteenth-century Renaissance. From the Enlightenment and the Age of Reason that followed, the modern era conducted a systematic assault on God. God was consigned to a smaller and smaller realm, occupying only the niches that could not be understood or explained by scientific inquiry. The freeing of people from ignorance was supposed to create a better world.

However, what modernity promised it failed to deliver. Despite the mantra that progress is better, human ills have diminished for only a portion of the human race. Age-old problems of disease, hunger, war, and injustice persist. The possibilities of nuclear annihilation, terrorist attack, or a pandemic viral outbreak render vulnerable even those ensconced behind citadels of wealth. Current institutions and systems are no longer trusted as adequate to deal with the growing complexities of the planet's dilemmas. The result is that people have turned again to transcendent belief systems to help them make sense of the world and its challenges.

God is back, big time! And he's breaking out of the box—the box that moderns tried to put him in. He's making his presence known beyond the confines of religion. He is showing up across all domains of culture. This means that people are not confining their search for God to traditional church settings. In addition, the pervasive mistrust of institutions characteristic of postmodern culture extends to institutional religion. Many people are conducting their search for spiritual vitality in the street, outside the church.

The 2008 Religious Landscape Survey conducted and published by the Pew Forum on Religion and Public Life discovered that the fastest-growing segment of religious affiliation in the country is the nonaffiliated (16.1 percent of adults age eighteen and older).[3] People moving into the unaffiliated category outnumber those moving out by greater than a 3-to-1 margin. Throughout the 1980s and 1990s, this percentage of unaffiliated Americans had held between 5 and 8 percent, meaning that this group has more than doubled in the past decade. One of the more instructive findings in the study, from my point of view, is that 25 percent of all adults under age thirty are now in the unaffiliated category. While only one-fourth of the religiously unaffiliated classify themselves as atheists or agnostic (1.6 and 2.4 percent, respectively), half of the other respondents in this category say that religion is important or very important in their lives. Clearly, the move away from affiliation is not a move away from God. It does signal a disaffection for the institutional church that is changing the spiritual landscape drastically—and quickly.

All this calls for an expression of Christian spirituality that does not reflect or rely on the Constantinian world order for its major self-understanding. After Constantine, Christianity became a clergy-dominated religion centered around designated places of worship. This differed radically from its first three centuries. The movement founded by Jesus was largely a marketplace phenomenon, an organic connection among people who were experiencing a way of life together. The early days of the movement focused on simple teachings of Jesus, with particular attention to living lives of sacrifice and service to one another and to one's neighbor. Even though the movement spread very rapidly among the slave populations and common people, its appeal transcended all cultural lines. The spiritual expression of Jesus followers was not characterized by a set of religious activities layered on top of other interests. Jesus invaded all areas of life. Church was not an event or a place; it was a way of life. It must become a way of life again. Enter the missional church.

## Missional Shift 3: From Church-Based to Kingdom-Based Leadership

Today's spiritual realities call for the third shift of the missional renaissance, from church-based to kingdom-based leadership. The spirituality the world needs must be robust enough to engage people where they live, work, and play. This kingdom movement requires spiritual leaders who understand the culture's search for God and who are willing to engage this discussion. These leaders do not insist or depend on people's leaving their own turf behind to have this conversation. They do not need the props of religious authority or church real estate to pursue their passion of introducing people to the revelation of God's heart for the world through Jesus. Their agenda differs significantly from those leaders who see their major task as serving people who come to church.

Accomplishing the first two shifts demanded by the missional renaissance will take a kind of leadership geared toward stimulating and supporting a movement. Much of the kingdom movement agenda will be focused outside the "organized" church, exercising its influence in the world beyond the church by bringing church into every domain of the culture. This does not mean that missional leaders cannot serve in the institutional church. But it does mean that if they do fill a traditional church role, they conduct it with a missional agenda. The content and character of their leadership will be very different from others who hold similar positions but view their responsibilities through a church-based mind-set.

Missional leaders are thinking differently about what church could be and even should be. The difference in their thinking is measured not in degree but in kind. For these leaders, church has moved from being internally occupied to externally focused, from primarily concentrating on its institutional maintenance to developing an incarnational influence. These leaders find themselves thinking of kingdom impact more than church growth. These innovators (twenty-first-century apostles and prophets) are imagining the church as a catalyst to mobilize all the community, synergizing the altruistic impetus, to work on the big things that God cares about. Their agenda stands in stark contrast to the program-driven church of the modern era. Their devotion to God is lived out in their determination to bless and to develop people who are made in his image.

This leadership shift will cull many present church leaders whose lips profess that they want to go missional but do not have it in their hearts. In an extended treatment of this shift that comes later in the book, we will explore some of the challenges inherent in making this leadership shift. Spiritual leaders will not only have to see their roles differently; they will also have to demonstrate in their lives what it is they want people to do. This may require that they acquire new competencies for an assignment that is quite different from managing a church role. The training agenda for leaders of movements differs quite dramatically from the current leadership training models in place for readying clergy to lead churches. These leaders will also have to answer the question of the proper role of clergy in a missional church. Many are probably going to have to raise financial support for themselves and for their ministries. And in the process of doing all this, missional church leaders are going to have the time of their lives.

## What's Next?

There are two things, then, I want to accomplish in these pages. First, I want to explore these three distinctive shifts that characterize the missional renaissance in terms of theology and practice, thinking and behavior. I will offer some language to capture and to express these implications for the church and for spiritual leaders. This discussion will not only help you think this through yourself but will also help you communicate with others what must be done to engage the missional renaissance. It is my hope that these pages will become powerful ways of convincing and recruiting others to join your journey. But be careful—once you start down this path, it will ruin you to the old world. You will be faced with choice after choice that will serve to declare your intentions about whether or not you will engage the missional renaissance.

Second, I also want to suggest what a new missional church scorecard might consist of. We need a new scorecard to support the rise of the missional church in North America. A universal maxim of human behavior—in families, at school, at work, wherever—is that what gets rewarded gets done. This means that the old church scorecard of how many, how often, how much—all bottom-line measures that are calculated in terms of church activity—is counterproductive to participating in the missional renaissance. The old scorecard keeps us church-absorbed. As long as we use it, we will continue to be inward-focused, program-driven, and church-based in our thinking and leadership.

Missional church is not about "doing church" better—at least, not the way we've "done church" in North America. It is not church growth in a new dress. It is not adding a smoke machine for the worship center or hiring a new band. It is not about church renewal, which generally means trying to find some new way to revitalize the troops to do church better with the hope of poofing up the numbers as the end result. Missional church is not a fad, the next big thing. Missional thinking and living change the game completely. The missional renaissance is altering both the character and the expression of the church in the world.

Ours is an age that celebrates in fresh ways the potential of people to make a difference, just as the original Renaissance reawakened the human spirit to noble pursuits. This outpouring of good and hope in the face of so many daunting challenges, together with people's desire to grow and to experience genuine spiritual vitality, represents the spiritual awakening of our times.

The missional renaissance reflects the church's response in a time of a remarkable manifestation of the kingdom. Those who miss it will find themselves on the other side of a divide that renders them irrelevant to the movement of God in the world. Those who engage it will find themselves at the intersection of God's redemptive mission and the world he loves so much he was willing to die for it.

# 2

# MISSIONAL MANIFESTO

He kept pressing me for an answer: "Tell me what a missional church is." My inquisitor was a fellow presenter at a national gathering of church leaders. He was intent on my describing what a missional church looks like. I tried to explain why we weren't getting very far in our conversation. "When you refer to 'a' missional church, you miss the point," I said. "The discussion should be about 'the' church. 'A' church is an institutional way of looking at church. 'The' church is a movement. 'The' church is people." He didn't buy it. My answer didn't satisfy his need to develop a description of a something he wanted to call "church."

This encounter reveals different points of departure in how people view the church. These are not just points in tension; they are irreconcilable in their implications for what people wind up thinking and doing. When we use *a* instead of *the* in front of *church*, I think we miss the missional revolution in its true essence, by reverting to language supporting institutional implications. "A" church draws on centuries of thinking about a corporate something that exists apart from the people who make it up. This language fails to make the break with the Western, Constantinian, institutional view of what church is. Missional followers of Jesus don't *belong* to a church. They *are* the church. Wherever *they* are, the church is present. Church is not something outside of themselves that they go to or join or support; it's something they *are*.

The missional church is not a *what* but a *who*. When we think of church in *what* mode, we focus on something that exists apart from people, some "out there" that people join and attend and support. We try, then, to build great churches, believing that this is God's primary strategy to engage the world. Inevitably, this pre-occupation leads to discussions of how we can "do church" better. Thinking about church in *who* mode focuses on what it means to be the people of God. The central task is developing great followers of Jesus, believing that God has created people to demonstrate his redemptive intentions to the world in and through them. This perspective frames an agenda so that the community of faith may encourage all its members to be faithful to God and to his mission as they live out being the church *in the world*.

This chapter offers a missional manifesto, a characterization of the missional church that helps us see it as God sees it and informs us about what should occupy its attention. Declaring what the missional church is requires us to do some theological reflection, not just cultural exegesis. Although the social trends noted in Chapter One have set up the environment for the missional renaissance, they did not create the missional church. God did that. The cultural questions merely anticipate God's answer to them. So our task is theological.

The following discussion explores missional theology along several lines. We will look at how some missional thinkers express what the missional church means to them. We will then examine some key biblical underpinnings of missional thought. Finally, we will explore significant underlying assumptions that shape and guide missional church thinking.

## The Heart of the Missional Church

The missional church is an expression of God's heart. It serves as an indication of his continuing commitment to his redemptive mission in the world. Because God is on mission, the people of

God are too. God is a sending God. Just as he sent his Son and his Holy Spirit to the world, he is sending his people into the world. All sendings share the same redemptive mission. The notion of "sentness" lies at the heart of the missional church because it reveals the heart of God.

The theologian Darrell Guder sums it up this way:

> Mission is the result of God's initiative, rooted in God's purposes to restore and heal creation. "Mission" means "sending," and it is the central biblical theme describing the purpose of God's action in human history. God's mission began with the call of Israel to receive God's blessings in order to be a blessing to the nations. God's mission unfolded in the history of God's people across the centuries recorded in Scripture, and it reached its revelatory climax in the incarnation of God's work of salvation in Jesus ministering, crucified, and resurrected. God's mission continued then in the sending of the Spirit to call forth and empower the church as the witness to God's good news in Jesus Christ.[1]

Another theologian, David Bosch, like many others, sees in this idea of sending a reflection of the very nature of God. "Mission [is] understood as being derived from the very nature of God. It [is] thus put in the context of the doctrine of the Trinity, not of ecclesiology or soteriology. The classical doctrine of the *missio Dei* as God the Father sending the Son, and God the Father and the Son sending the Spirit, [is] expanding to include yet another 'movement': Father, Son, and Holy Spirit sending the church into the world."[2]

The *mission Dei* is redemptive. It anticipates not only the prayer that Jesus taught his followers to pray, that the will of God would be done on earth as it is in heaven, but that we would be involved in God's response. "A missional church is a church that is shaped by participating in God's mission, which is to set things right in a broken, sinful world, to redeem it, and to restore it to what God has always intended for the world."[3]

God's mission has been most clearly revealed in the Incarnation. The missional church is inextricably bound to Jesus, pointing people to him.

> By its witness—in word and deed and common life—to the centrality of the work of Jesus in his ministry, death, and resurrection it offers to all people the possibility of understanding that the meaning and goal of history are not to be found in any of the projects, programs, ideologies, and utopias which offer themselves in competition with one another; . . . but that it is to be found in a person and a history which breaks decisively through this endless succession by breaching the final barrier of death and opening a new horizon for human affairs.[4]

The problem is that the Western church veered away from this self-understanding as rooted in God's mission and assumed other agendas. George Hunsberger, in "Sizing Up the Shape of the Church," offers a taxonomy of what people view the nature of the church to be. He argues that one's understanding of the church becomes determinative for the church's agenda. Hunsberger identifies three distinct notions of church that people have in mind when they think about what the church is. While the definitions that follow are his, the commentary is mine to shape his observations for use in our discussion.[5]

From the Reformation heritage comes the understanding of the church as "a place where certain things happen." What these "certain things" are varies from tradition to denominational tribe, but they include activities along the lines of preaching and teaching the Bible, observing sacraments, and engaging in worship. What happens "at the church" and how it happens, including doctrinal differences and nuances, establish people's view of their own church and how it differs from other churches.

This view of the church seems to operate predominantly when the culture is Christianized. The assumption is that Christian values permeate all of society, so one goes to church to perform certain rites and then goes on with life in a way that will not be challenged by a hostile culture or deemed at odds with a Christian worldview and practice. This is how church was viewed throughout much of Christian history after Constantine.

Hunsberger identifies a second view of church in which it is seen as "a vendor of religious goods and services." Though this seems a crass way to put it, I think it is an apt description of the program church. Members and participants expect the church to provide a range of services, from favorite music and fellowship options to sports leagues and travel opportunities. In this view, other churches actually become competitors in the religious marketplace for the energy, money, and affiliation of people they can attract and keep satisfied through the services they offer.

A third view of the nature of the church, Hunsberger suggests, is seeing the church as "a body of people sent on a mission." My question is, Whose mission is it? Lots of churches see themselves on a mission. They have carefully articulated mission statements, often having spent great energy developing them and making sure everyone understands them. The dilemma is that these congregations often wind up inventing something that does not reflect the heart of God. Then they ask God to bless them in their efforts, a mission that he had no hand in framing and has no heart for.

The missional church believes it is God who is on mission and that we are to join him in it. As Bishop Leslie Newbigin says, "It seems to me to be of great importance to insist that mission is not first of all an action of ours. It is an action of God."[6] Our job, then, is to do what the Baptist thinker Henry Blackaby often suggests: find out what God is doing and join him in it.

When the church understands itself from this point of view, it offers a corrective to the first two views. Anticipating some of the themes in this book, Michael Frost and Alan Hirsch identify some of the deconstruction implicit in the missional church:

> The missional church . . . will be an anticlone of the existing traditional model. [First,] rather than being attractional, it will be incarnational. It will leave its own religious zones and live

comfortably with non-church-goers, seeping into the host culture like salt and light. It will be an infiltrating, transformational community. Second, rather than being dualistic, it will embrace a messianic spirituality, . . . a spirituality of engagement with culture and the world in the same mode as the Messiah himself. And third, the missional church will develop an apostolic form of leadership rather than the traditional hierarchical model.[7]

## A Missional Characterization

So how do we pull all this together in coming to an understanding of what the missional church is? My answer is that <u>the missional church is *the people of God partnering with God in his redemptive mission in the world*</u>. This understanding of the church is both liberating and sobering. It is liberating in the sense that we realize we don't have to manufacture the work of God in ourselves or in the world. God is doing the heavy lifting! This means we can quit trying to drum up a breeze by generating a lot of frenetic church activity and instead hoist our sails to catch the breeze that's already blowing.

At the same time, this understanding of *who* we are as the church (not *what* we are—a place or a religious vendor) carries great responsibility. <u>Our job is not to "do church" well but to be the people of God in an unmistakable way in the world</u>. We are to be the aroma of Jesus in the cemetery of decaying flesh. We are to be different in the hope we offer, in the grace we exhibit, and in the obvious sacrifice of love we display in dealing with others.

This characterization of what the missional church is allows for its organic expression because it describes the church in terms of people. This means that wherever missional followers of Jesus are, the church is there—at home, at work, at school, in the neighborhood, at the ballpark, in the dance studio, in the homeless shelter, at the airport—wherever followers of Jesus are taking seriously their identity as the people of God. Once when

I was sharing these views at a conference of collegiate ministers, a participant said, "You mean to tell me that if two Christians are tutoring high school students in English, that's a church?" My reply was that centuries of conditioning would lead us in the West to frame that question that way, in an attempt to define some organization so we can talk about it. "What I am saying," I explained, "is if people are tutoring students in the name of Jesus, *the church is there*."

Our "thereness" is what the world needs. It needs the church to be there, addressing every brokenness caused by sin, reflecting the heart of God to the world as partners in *his redemptive mission*. This is a way of "seeing" church that moves it past its institutional moorings and reengages its movement beginnings. We have been called out to be sent in, to "be there," *in the world*.

This characterization does not preclude corporate and organizational expressions of missional ministry. In fact, this book is written largely to help congregations and ministry organizations know what shifts they need to make to "go missional." But the characterization of the missional church I offer here anticipates and accommodates the reality that many Jesus followers may create their own expressions for missional living. Some will remain part of the institutional, traditional church. Others will create or be a part of distinct missional communities focused on encouraging one another to intentional life as a Jesus follower. Still other missional Jesus followers will live out their missional expression in the marketplace or in some life hobby where they spend a good deal of time and have built significant relationships.

There is no need to hear in this characterization a licensing of privatized and individual spiritual life. The biblical designation of what it means to be the people of God is always plural. It implies and insists on community. This again reflects the very nature of God, who exists in perfect community as a Trinity. The missional follower of Jesus cannot conceive of their spiritual identity outside of being in accountable and encouraging relationships with other Jesus followers. Church is not a part of life for the missional Jesus follower; it is a way of life with others who are on a similar journey.

The missional life shows up in every endeavor, because the church has been sent by God into the world to reflect his heart for the world. This is what it means to be on mission with God, *partnering with God*. It is not a mission that is pursued as something added to daily life, something outside the normal range of activity, a quest to do something beyond your life's assignments. It is a way of seeing oneself as partnering with God in daily life, executing the mundane as well as pursuing the sublime, with an intentionality of blessing people and sharing the life of God with them.

## The Bible for Missional Eyes

Many of us have had the experience at the optometrist's office of sitting through the lens-flipping exercise to determine the right prescription for our glasses and contacts. With a singe lens change, objects that were blurry or even unseen can become visible and crisp. The lens change didn't create the letters. They were there all along. Nor did the new prescription eliminate anything already seen. The correct lens just opens up a richer field of vision.

Similarly, once you flip kingdom lenses into place, you begin to see things in the biblical witness you've never seen before. The missional perspective views the Bible through a much different lens than the glasses many church people have been wearing. As one pastor said to me, "Suddenly I'm seeing this missional stuff everywhere in scripture. It's like, how could I have missed this all along?" It was his conversion to missional that had given him sight.

In a church-centric world, the Bible is viewed as God's self-revealing gift to his people, chronicling for them his work on their behalf and how they are to conduct their lives together as his people. In this context, Bible study typically functions as a devotional aid and an instructive lesson applied to church people who find what they need for godly living. The Bible certainly does all this, but there is much more there for the missional follower of Jesus. For the missional church, the Bible serves as a narrative to help the people of God understand his mission in the world and their role in it. It serves as an authoritative guide for living as God's people while being on mission with him to woo the world. It conveys God's hopes for humanity, his dreams of how people should treat one another and what life in the kingdom looks like. By forcing us to see the disparities between the kingdoms of this earth and the kingdom of God, it becomes far more disruptive than informational. The Bible presents a call to action, not just a lesson to be studied.

The following Scripture selections demonstrate how a missional perspective enriches our understanding and application of biblical truth. These portions are not meant to be exhaustive but serve to illustrate the Scriptural moorings of the missional church.

> The Lord had said to Abram . . . "I will make you
> into a great nation, and I will bless you; I will make
> your name great, and you will be a blessing. . . .
> And all peoples on earth will be blessed through
> you."
>
> *Genesis 12:1–3*

In this remarkable exchange, God offers an Aramaean chieftain incredible privilege and responsibility. God chooses to bless Abraham with an end in mind. His ultimate endeavor is to bless the world through Abraham. This simple but far-reaching covenant means that the people of God are charged with the responsibility and enjoy the privilege to bless everyone. God chose to embody his blessing in a people who were to show the world who he is and what he wants them to enjoy.

Melchizedek, Jethro, Jonah, Jesus—what ties these biblical names and their stories together? For the missional church, they make the point that God is always at work beyond his people, people of Abraham's line.

As the metanarrative of Genesis 12 continues to unfold throughout the Bible, so does the reminder that Abraham's story is not the only story being told. Melchizedek is a priest of God contemporary with Abraham who instructs Abraham, so apparently God was talking to more people than one chieftain. Jesus is called a high priest after the order of Melchizedek (not Aaron, as the author of Hebrews elaborates), sealing the point that Jesus is high priest over the whole world, not just one particular group of people.

Jethro plays a huge role in the Exodus saga, the biggest event in Old Testament history. On top of giving Moses a wife and a job when the prince is a fugitive, Jethro intervenes with good administrative advice when Moses' leadership challenges threatened to overwhelm him. Jethro was certainly not part of the Abrahamic line. He was a Midianite and yet a priest of God. So how did Jethro get cut in on the action? He had met God before he met Moses. Obviously, God was working with people beyond his people—helping to write the story of the people of God!

Jonah is told by God to go and deliver a message to the people of Nineveh. Not only were these ancient Assyrians not people of the line; they were the enemies of Israel! Yet God intended to get a message to them. Jonah does not express much enthusiasm for the mission, as you might recall. Instead he plays out the story of Old Testament Israel: he refuses his role in the mission of God; he is swallowed up in captivity; when released, he reluctantly obeys; then he pouts when God blesses other people. In a scene full of pathos, God reveals his motives and character. He in effect asks the prophet, "How could I not care about one hundred thousand people?" Even if Jonah didn't care, God did! Through this story, God instructs and reminds his people that he is working his redemptive mission even among the enemies of the people of God, not so they will be nice to God's people but because they are in his heart.

Jesus' birth and boyhood play out beyond the people of God. His entrance into the world seems better understood by people outside of Israel than those on the inside. "Where is the newborn king of the Jews?" is posed by Babylonians. Then Jesus is sheltered as a boy in Egypt. Babylon and Egypt—two empires that had enslaved the people of God in the Old Testament! Yet God chooses to give them big roles in the central drama of redemption. During his public ministry, Jesus made heroes of another unlikely group—Samaritans—even targeting them on mission excursions. Samaritans were certainly not considered a legitimate part of the line. And when Jesus announced that people not from Abraham were going to have a seat at the table in the kingdom, the Pharisees went ballistic. They rightfully understood that Jesus meant to wreck their religion. Even though they conspired to kill him, they couldn't stop him. They didn't stand a chance! God was continuing in Jesus what he had been up to all along—working out his redemptive mission in the world.

> Now if you obey me fully and keep my covenant,
> then out of all nations you will be my treasured
> possession. Although the whole earth is mine,
> you will be for me a kingdom of priests and a holy
> nation. These are the words you are to speak to the
> Israelites.
>
> *Exodus 19:5–6*

> But you are a chosen people, a royal priesthood, a
> holy nation, a people belonging to God, that you
> may declare the praises of him who called you out
> of darkness into his wonderful light.
>
> *1 Peter 2:9*

These passages from the Old and New Testaments are often used to characterize the special nature of being God's people.

They reveal a key plank of God's strategy to engage humanity with his redemptive mission. Peter uses the imagery of Moses' dramatic Sinai encounter to demonstrate that God's determination to have a covenant people had not changed but had been transferred to the followers of Jesus. He has created a people to serve as his ongoing incarnational presence on the earth. God's people reveal his heart to the world by declaring God's person and story to the world and by demonstrating a way of life he intended people to enjoy.

> For God so loved the world that he gave his one
> and only Son, that whoever believes in him shall
> not perish but have eternal life.
>
> *John 3:16*

Jesus shocked Nicodemus with this statement. The Pharisee would have expected a much different mission of God. "For God so loved the *church*" would have been his take on it. Imagine the jarring disorientation experienced by the religious leader. First was the assertion that God has a Son, with all its obvious challenges to the radical monotheism central to the core belief of Judaism. Second was Jesus' declaration that the redemptive mission of God had the world in its crosshairs. For Pharisees like Nicodemus, the kingdom of God was seen as a reward intended for the benefit of God's people, not as a gift to the world. Church-centric thinking often still mirrors this same myopic and distorted view of God's missional heart.

> Jesus replied: "'Love the Lord your God with all
> your heart and with all your soul and with all your
> mind.' This is the first and greatest commandment.
> And the second is like it: 'Love your neighbor as
> yourself.' All the Law and the Prophets hang on
> these two commandments."
>
> *Matthew 22:37–40*

Missional followers of Jesus take seriously Jesus' claim that loving one's neighbor ranks right up there with loving God. They see this as an obvious application of what it means to be a blessing people. In the Luke version of this teaching, Jesus illustrates his idea of loving one's neighbor with a story in which church people come off looking bad while an outside-the-line Samaritan displays the heart of God. Among the lessons here is that substituting religious activity for helping people doesn't cut it with God. And shocking to the monocultural Pharisees of Jesus' day, kingdom values aren't exclusively reserved for or practiced by God's people. For God, it always counts when people love their neighbors, no matter who is doing it. The kingdom of God plays out with every act of compassion.

> I have come that they may have life, and have it to
> the full.
>
> *John 10:10b*

Jesus can't describe his mission any plainer than this. He wants to help people get a life! Those hearing this promise did not receive it as a statement characterizing future bliss. They knew it was about here and now. Jesus went about practicing the abundant life in full view of everyone. His kind of living substituted service for self-aggrandizement and trumped self-absorption by paying attention to others' needs. Jesus proved that this approach to life paves the way to abundance. Missional followers of Jesus adopt his example to live lives that are full-filled, not just filled full.

> Speaking the truth in love, we will in all things
> grow up into him who is the Head, that is, Christ.
>
> *Ephesians 4:13*

This statement was made by the apostle Paul to demonstrate what spiritual maturity looks like and what it accomplishes.

In fact, he characterized "speaking the truth in love" as a mark of the real church.

Missional followers of Jesus believe that both sides of this equation are important: truth and love. Mainline denominations and other ministries have been practicing a "social gospel" for decades, emphasizing love that involves ministries of justice and mercy and compassion. However, as one mainline leader confessed to me, "We have just been too afraid to mention Jesus." Evangelicals, on the other hand, have insisted on capital-T Truth and have sought to preserve and defend biblical truth against all comers. The trouble is that such devotion to being right has come off as self-righteousness to many people in our culture, especially in light of so little action on behalf of marginalized people in our society. Both approaches come up short. The missional movement understands that both truth and love must be present to reflect the whole heart of God for people. Not telling people the truth doesn't serve them fully even if you love them. Telling people the truth without loving them hardly encourages them to embrace it. Improving people's lives cannot just be seen as a prelude to evangelism. On the other hand, people need the truth of God's insights in order to be fully blessed.

> Always be prepared to give an answer to everyone
> who asks you to give the reason for the hope that
> you have.
>
> *1 Peter 3:15b*

This verse is a favorite among missional Jesus followers because it anticipates the dynamic that occurs when the people of God act like the people of God not because of our sermons but because of our service to them. The act of blessing people frequently leads them to inquire something along the lines of "Why are you doing this?" Having your motives questioned is music to the ears of someone prepared for it. "I am a follower of Jesus, and I am blessing you because that's what he came to do."

This answer opens the door for spiritual conversation. The verse assumes that we are being asked this question. The problem with North American Christianity is that our lack of loving service has precluded the opportunity for this exchange. I agree with a friend of mine who says that demonstration has replaced proclamation as the way to gain a hearing for the gospel.

> You are the salt of the earth. But if the salt loses
> its saltiness, how can it be made salty again? It is
> no longer good enough for anything, except to be
> thrown out and trampled by men. You are the light
> of the world. A city on a hill cannot be hidden.
> Neither do people light a lamp and put it under a
> bowl. Instead they put it on its stand, and it gives
> light to everyone in the house. In the same way, let
> your light shine before men, that they may see your
> good deeds and praise your Father in heaven.
>
> *Matthew 5:13–15*

It is impossible for missional Jesus followers to read these verses without a quickened heartbeat. These powerful metaphors show us what it means to be the people of God in the world. Salt penetrates, permeates, and preserves. All of these functions require its presence. It is not a neutral presence. Salt is an active ingredient that changes the flavor of things. The light metaphor illustrates the obvious truth that light shines in darkness. But it also adds the additional promise that when the people of God act like the people of God, we actually help people see God. In this teaching, Jesus raises the specter that when the people of God fail at their task, something significant is lost. The people of God lose their value, and people in the world fail to see God.

> As the Father has sent me, I am sending you.
>
> *John 20:21b*

This fascinating post-Resurrection encounter dramatically captures the genesis of the missional church. In this version of John's Great Commission, the apostle records a simple commissioning of Jesus: go! Jesus tags the church as a "sent people." Church people often focus on being "called out" as a command to come inside from the world. A refuge theology and practice betrays this understanding. Missional followers of Jesus understand they are being called out all right—called outside. They understand that Incarnation implies sentness, a going, because that's how Jesus described his own mission. He is the one sent, sent from God, conducting forays into the kingdom of darkness with his kingdom of light. His followers are to follow the same trajectory.

## The Plot Thickens

In the movies *Groundhog Day* and *50 First Dates*, the characters live the same day over and over again until something happens to change the endless loop of repetition. At that point, they have the opportunity to delve into a new chapter of life.

I might argue that for centuries, the church has been repeating the same storyline. The good news is that we have entered a new chapter. Elements of earlier plot developments remain in play, but new storylines are creating exciting new twists and turns. Even though we have confidence in the final outcome, we have never been this way before.

The missional church's story sees the human drama and God saga intertwined, one incomprehensible without the other. The following plot elements have helped give it shape. As the story heats up in the days ahead, these will be the themes we take forward as reference points for what God is up to, how we figure into the story, and how we need to play our part.

*People are created in the image of God.* People matter to God by virtue of their being created in his image. They are intentional acts of creation by a loving God. They therefore matter to the people of God. People deserve to be blessed simply because they are people, not just so we can "witness" to them.

*God is on mission.* The pre-Fall era displayed the God-human relationship as one of intimate engagement. Ever since the disruption of this caused by sin, God has proactively inserted himself into the drama to woo humankind back into intimate relationship with him. His search, commencing with Adam in the Garden, has been relentless throughout history, despite humanity's best efforts to hide from him. The supreme missional activity of God centers on his activity in Jesus, an unexpected Incarnation to demonstrate both full divine commitment to humanity and full human potential when lived completely connected with God. God is still on mission. Through every human experience, his Spirit seeks to draw people out of hiding and into relationship with him.

*God's mission is redemptive.* The welfare of people created in his image captures the heart and imagination of God. He wants to restore not just the nature of his intended relationship with people but the benefits of it as well. Adequate food, restorative rest, authentic relationships, life in harmony with the rest of the created order, health, meaningful work, peace, security—these are blessings that God granted in the Garden and still wants humanity to experience. Supremely, God desires restoration in the relationship he intended with human beings. Whatever threatens these conditions and this relationship causes him grief and earns his wrath. Sin steals life. Jesus wars against life robbers in his life, death, and Resurrection. He declared that he had come to give life, life to the full. This means that missional Jesus followers are engaged in all aspects of human experience—political, social, economic, cultural, physical, psychological, and spiritual—to work for those things that enhance life and to oppose those things that steal life.

*God's mission is always being prosecuted in the world.* I use the term *world* here to refer to all human beings, not just those who are part of the group we know as the people of God. God has not limited his mission to acting only on behalf of people who know and love him. His efforts can't be shrink-wrapped down to church issues or activity. The kingdom, the realm of God's rule, is way bigger than the church.

*God doesn't postpone his mission, waiting for the church to "get it."* When it comes to new spiritual frontiers and breakthroughs, the church often lags behind the Spirit. The subtext of the first half of the Book of Acts is the church playing catch-up to the Spirit. Even though the disciples had accompanied Jesus to the village of Sychar in Samaria, been sent to other Samaritan villages on other mission trips, and heard Jesus describe neighborly love with a story involving a Samaritan, they were still shocked when the Spirit visited Samaritans with their own Pentecost. Then it got even wilder—the Spirit extended Pentecost to the Gentiles! The missional church movement recognizes that the Spirit is at work in extraordinary ways. Not wanting to be left behind, missional followers of Jesus are running to catch up.

*God is up to something new.* The missional church reflects a new conversation that God is having with us about the nature of the church and its role in the world. God's conversations always change things, often dramatically. His conversation with Abraham reshaped the spiritual landscape of human history. His face-to-face meetings with Moses revealed his heart for his people. God's dialogues with Paul captured the heart of the Pharisee and imbued the Christian movement with a missionary spirit. And ever since the Word became flesh, the conversation about God has never been the same. He is now having a new conversation with the church. Almost every week, when I speak, someone comes up during a break and asks me if I've read so-and-so or met so-and-so because "the two of you are saying the same thing." Often I haven't read the book or met the person. I usually laugh and tell them, "We're just working from the same Source!" People who've never communicated with each other are thinking the same thoughts and taking the same actions. Scales are falling from people's eyes. The Spirit is speaking across the distributive network he has had in place since Pentecost.

*The people of God play an important role in the mission of God.* In the metanarrative that has its origins in the deal that he struck with Abraham, God created a people to be his partner in his redemptive mission. In that exchange, God initiates a covenantal relationship, meaning that the people of God have responsibilities to *be* the people of God. And there are consequences when the people of God fail in their covenantal relationship. The biblical record often observes that when the people of God mistakenly think they are God's only or primary concern, they become callous to the very people God is wooing. This attitude reflects poorly on God and earns his judgment. Jesus' beef with the Pharisees focused precisely on their failure on this point. They misrepresented his Father while claiming to be his representatives on earth. The church that claims to be the people of God must submit itself to the role of participating in the mission of God in the world. The very notion that the church can be successful apart from an improved world reflects a disconnect from God's mission and even raises the question of whether or not people who think this way are even recognized by God as his people.

*The kingdom is a future that provokes a crisis.* The missional church movement reflects a new dimension of kingdom advance, an intensified outbreak. This produces a crisis for those who encounter it, just as it did in the days when Jesus walked the planet. People, including leaders of churches, are being confronted with a choice of whether or not they will enter the kingdom. Once they do, the old world will increasingly become alien to them, causing further disruption between their life and ministry agenda and the preoccupations of those enmeshed in the church-age worldview. Kingdom agents have no other option than being subversive, attempting to introduce kingdom realities to every domain of life and culture, even the church.

*The missional expression of church will require new metrics to measure its vitality.* The current scorecard for the North American church is tied to the definitions of church as a place and church as a vendor of religious goods and services. Merely assessing church activity does not adequately reflect the missional dimensions of joining God's work in the world. Since people are generally motivated by doing what gets rewarded, the development of a missional scorecard is critical. This scorecard will, by its existence, educate people to new possibilities, resulting in new behaviors and even greater movement toward missional expressions of Christianity.

*Missional expression can grow out of the current church, but it is not limited to the current church.* The missional agenda literally just requires that Jesus followers live missionally. People currently immersed in nonmissional religious church systems can begin to practice missional Christianity. Some are keeping their church membership or even their leadership roles while they are making the transition. Some do not choose that path. They are creating other ways of living their faith, some in missional communities and others in marketplace expression. Some serve as missionaries to the church as part of the wooing strategy of God. While these prophetic messengers are often viewed as threatening (to those who should be threatened), they are another sign of God's grace in restoring his people to their rightful covenantal relationship with him and his intention to continue working through his church to prosecute his redemptive mission in the world.

## Shifting into Missional Mode

The missional church is the people of God partnering with God in his redemptive mission in the world. This characterization intentionally allows for a wide range of expression, as wide as God's interaction. Missional is not a place you arrive at but a direction in which you are moving. It is a way of being in the world.

So what specifically do you need to do to move into the missional movement?

If you want to go missional, you need to make three major shifts. In the pages that follow, we will explore each of these.

You will need to intentionally nurture these shifts if you want to make missional progress. A new scorecard will help you adopt the actions and behaviors necessary to pursue this missional agenda. Accordingly, we will consider what that new scorecard might include.

Are you ready to go missional? Let's get started.

# 3

# MISSIONAL SHIFT 1: FROM AN INTERNAL TO AN EXTERNAL FOCUS

I opened the e-mail newsletter as soon as it landed in my inbox. Since I had known the leaders of the new congregation for years, I was curious to check on their progress. In their one-year reflection edition, there was a noticeable lack of typical church stats, such as weekly worship attendance and offerings. The lone number in the report was startling, however. It was the number 3,000. That is the number of community service hours logged by volunteers in service projects in their first year. These projects ranged from cleaning up playgrounds and painting schools to rescuing a homeowner from foreclosure and building a school in Iraq. The home page of my friends' new congregational Web site states that their church's vision is to love God and love others in profound ways. They were willing to stake the "evidence of this vision" as being "seen through our demonstrated acts of service." It looks to me that they are delivering!

In a follow-up phone conversation with their community service director, I learned that most of the people involved in these projects are not Jesus followers. Yet they are being introduced to a whole new expression of church: the externally focused church. Rick Rusaw and my colleague Eric Swanson coined this term in their wonderful book, *The Externally Focused Church*.[1]

When most people think about going missional, this kind of activity and emphasis is what they imagine. They picture shifting ministries from an internal to an external focus, meaning some kind of community activity or involvement. Unfortunately, many church leaders think that simply their engagement in some kind of community service makes them missional. But that's not the case. That would reduce what it means to be missional to just being another program or methodological approach to "doing church." It misses the point.

The shift from an internal to an external focus signals more than an emphasis or an activity; it is a tectonic shift. It involves changing the very understanding of what the church is, not just what it does, though that changes dramatically as well. Moving to an external focus pushes the church from doing missions as some second-mile project into being on mission as a way of life.

If this distinction still seems a little unclear, it may help to examine some of the many thinking and behavioral aspects of the shift that are involved in making this transition from internal to external. No single part of the shift captures all that the entire movement entails; however, viewed together, they begin to give shape to this particular aspect of missional personality that expands the horizons of what the church is. You might also find that these descriptions serve to create a language for communicating this shift to others in your faith community.

## From Church-Centric to Kingdom-Focused

The shift from the church at the center to the kingdom of God at the center is the theological and philosophical underpinning of the move from an internal to an external focus. It can be likened to the radical adjustment in thinking that occurred when it was discovered that the sun, not the earth, was at the center of the solar system. The resulting shift from a Ptolemaic worldview to a Copernican universe required a recalibration of the place of our planet in the larger scheme of things, not just what space it occupied.

Similarly, the church has occupied center stage in the minds of church people for centuries. In this worldview, God's redemptive mission focused his work on creating a people to serve him. The crosshairs of God's love lined up squarely on the church, which was his primary concern on earth throughout history.

This view had the effect of shrink-wrapping God's activity in the world down to the church. In this system of thought, God preferred hanging out at church with his people. The idea of what it meant to be Christian became synonymous with what it meant to be a committed church person. Further, the measure of personal devotion to God was the degree of one's separation from the world outside the church. This meant centering one's life on the church and its activities, usually pulling away from people who weren't willing to do the same. The primary focus of evangelism was converting people to the church culture.

Church life was also affected by this view. Churches measured their effectiveness by how much church activity they could generate. Churches built schools and day-care centers, followed by health clubs and radio stations—whatever it took to be a "full-service" church (yes, that term was actually used by church consultants and in church growth literature). Church leaders became convinced that "successful" churches would capture the attention of pagans (nonchurchgoers), who would then come and turn their lives over to God and to the church.

This perspective also affected the church's view of its relationship to the world beyond the church. An entire parallel culture was created so that Christians wouldn't have to venture out much into that world. Attending church helped church people "make it through the week" until they could get back to church. People in the church were told to "take God with them" as they left church. Ideally, they worked alongside, went to school with, and lived next door to neighbors who were also committed church people. And God's work in the world all depended on them. "There is no plan B" was the subject of many sermons exhorting church people to step up to their responsibility to convert people around them (which meant turning them into church people). We were to "reach" people with the gospel. "Reaching" people often meant that we cut them off from their previous relationships as we absorbed them into the church culture.

I grew up in this church-centric world. The result was that I viewed the kingdom through church eyes. The kingdom was primarily something that was going to be ushered in someday. "Thy kingdom come" was a prayer for the return of Jesus, who would finally set up a world where church people would feel at home. The closest thing to kingdom activity was when churches cooperated to do more church stuff—citywide revivals and joint worship services and such. Later on in my life, kingdom enterprise became synonymous with efforts of the church to take over the world through political means.

Rather than looking at the kingdom through church lenses, the missional church looks at the church through kingdom lenses. The missional church repudiates the church-centric views of God's work in the world and the church's relationship to the world.

In a kingdom-oriented worldview, the target of God's redemptive love is the world, not the church ("For God so loved the *world*," Jesus said; not "for God so loved the *church*"). This means that God is always at work in the world, not just in the church, prosecuting his redemptive mission. His efforts are not shrink-wrapped down to church activity, nor is he hamstrung in his progress by waiting for the church to join him in what he is doing.

In a missional approach, as the church engages the world, it finds Jesus, whose home is in the streets or wherever he has to go to connect with the people he is pursuing, meaning everybody. In a church-centric world, our responsibility is to bring people out of the streets into the church. A kingdom-oriented approach seeks to leverage the gospel into people's lives right where they live, work, and play. The church is wherever followers of Jesus are. People don't *go to* church; they *are* the church. They don't bring people to church; they bring the church to people.

## From Destination to Connector

I travel by plane almost every week. This means I get to visit a lot of airports. On a fairly routine basis, airports get confused about what they're there for—and for whom. They think that if a bunch of planes are on the ground, close to the hub, and the concourse is full of people, they are winning. They apparently think they are the destination! Of course, when this happens, it means a bunch of people aren't getting where they want to go. They're stuck at the airport, like flies on flypaper.

The airport is a place of connection, not a destination. Its job is to help people get somewhere else. An airport-centric world of travel would be dull and frustrating, no matter how nice the airport is.

When the church thinks it's the destination, it also confuses the scorecard. It thinks that if people are hovering around and in the church, the church is winning. The truth is, when that's the case, the church is really keeping people from where they want to go, from their real destination. That destination is life. Lucky for us, it just so happens this is what Jesus promised to bring to us. (He did not say, "I have come to give you *church* and give it to you more abundantly.") Abundant life is lived out with loved ones, friends, and acquaintances in the marketplace, in the home, in the neighborhood, in the world.

The church is a connector, linking people to the kingdom life that God has for them. Substituting church activity as the preferred life expression is as weird as believing that airports are more interesting than the destinations they serve.

# From Thinking We Are the Point to Being Absolutely the Point

Once when I was giving a talk about the differences between externally and internally focused churches, an obviously agitated pastor interrupted me to say, "I've always been taught that the church and the kingdom are the same thing." This is church-centric thinking in its most extreme form. He then launched into an animated monologue about how special the church is, weaving in biblical phrases about being the bride of Christ and the chosen people. After his highly emotional outburst, he left the room. He came back later, explaining that he just had to get away to "wrap his mind around" the concept that God might be doing something besides working on the church.

That pastor is not alone. A lot of people get nervous when we begin to consider the biblical teaching that challenges the idea that the church is the destination. They think that the result will be that the church loses its specialness in what God is doing on earth. That couldn't be further from the case, but they have to get past their cherished perspective that the church is the point. In fact, I often ask groups of people, "What's the point of being the people of God if the people of God are not the point?"

The role of the church is simply this: to bless the world. In doing this, the people of God reveal God's heart for the world.

To understand what it means to be the people of God, it's important to go all the way back to where their story got going. It is in Genesis 12, in the deal God cut with Abraham. In that God-initiated covenant, God didn't declare to Abraham, "I'm going to bless you, just you and people like you." Not at all. The point of that blessing was its external focus: "I'm going to bless you," God said, "so you can be a blessing to everybody else." This included people not in Abraham's tribe, people not like Abraham, people who didn't know God or were even looking for him—everybody, period.

The emphasis on the scope of this blessing highlights two things: the unlimited reach of the blessing and its unqualified nature. Followers of Jesus have inherited this blessing, meaning we are free to bless everyone and responsible for blessing everyone. This includes people like us and people not like us, people we like and people we don't like, people who share our values and people who don't. You get the point.

Frequently when I'm with congregations in a teaching or preaching venue, I call on them to quit evangelizing. I say this somewhat tongue in cheek but try to make two points with it. First, the church has turned evangelism into some kind of activity or program that we train people to engage in rather than recognizing evangelism as a natural by-product of a Jesus follower's life. When evangelism is a program, it often involves questionable methods that commoditize Jesus and Christianity and frequently involve some ploy to get people to connect to church. Second, people don't want to do it; if they did, we wouldn't have to work so hard to recruit them or guilt them into working on their evangelism efforts. We need a better alternative, and I think we have one.

Instead of having an evangelism strategy, I urge congregations and people to develop a blessing strategy. This advice is based on God's covenant with Abraham in Genesis 12 where he makes the point of what it means to be the people of God. I usually challenge them to "bless three people this week." Then, to drive home a truth, I add, "and make sure one of them doesn't deserve it!" Of course, none of us deserves it! That's the good news of the Good News—that we get the undeserved blessings of God. We don't own the blessings of God, and we sure don't get to decide who deserves them. The clear biblical teaching is that God blesses everyone because that's just who he is and what he likes to do.

What happens when God's people decide to live out their covenant to bless those around them? Pretty amazing stuff. Every week, I hear from someone who has come alive to this idea.

In some cases, it is people who decide to routinely bless wait staff in restaurants. In one case, the leader of a women's conference decided to release five hundred women into the streets of Chicago just to pray for people, resulting in some incredible encounters. Usually, when pastors tell me about being a blessing people, they comment on the new sense of life that permeates their gatherings as people share their stories. That makes sense, doesn't it? Once people start witnessing a few resurrections, everything else pales in comparison.

I received a series of three e-mails a couple of years ago from a guy who had attended a conference where I laid out my typical challenge for people to go out and intentionally bless people. His first informed me that he had decided to bless the baristas at Starbucks, since he went there every day. "I'll let you know how it goes," he concluded. His second e-mail told me that the staff at the coffeeshop thought it was a little strange when he asked them, "How can I ask God to bless you?" (That question was not random on his part. At the conference where he and I met, we had talked about using these words to open up spiritual conversations because they reflect the heart of God and the heart of the follower of Jesus.) However, even though they were initially reluctant to talk to him, the employees began to seek him out on their breaks, sit with him, and open up their lives to him. He had become so jazzed by their response that he had shared it with his small church group. They then discovered that as a group, they were customers of every Starbucks within a thirteen-block radius in their city. They decided they would each bless the baristas in all those shops when they went for coffee. E-mail three a few weeks later recounted an episode that had happened to him that day. Visiting a Starbucks that he didn't normally frequent, he asked his standard question when the barista handed him his cup of coffee, whereupon she pulled the cup back and said, "Are you one of those *blessing* people?"

When I read this, my spirit cried, "Yes, yes, *yes!*" That's exactly who we are. We are the people of God. We are the blessing people!

The act of blessing people carries both risks and rewards. People might just invite you into their pain once they know you care. But you will also be invited into their joy. One Jesus follower told me a story involving both pain and joy. He was shopping in a sporting goods store he frequents when he noticed that the manager seemed to be having a bad day. He decided to bless the man. When he approached the man and asked how his day was going, the man replied, "I wish I was anywhere but here." The shopper simply responded, "I will pray for you." This simple act of caring caused the man to blurt out his hurts. "I'm working over sixty hours a week, I'm losing money, and I've probably already lost my marriage. I don't know what to do." The Jesus follower said, "I'll ask God to help you." When he returned to the store a few days later, the manager flagged him down to share some good news: "I got an offer out of the blue to buy this store. I'm going to make money, and my wife's agreed to go to counseling." All this in four days! This is our God. He just loves to show up and show off!

To practice the blessing life, you will need to believe God, not just believe *in* God. There's a huge difference between the two. Abraham just didn't believe in God; he believed God—he staked his life on what God said. We have to believe that God has the ability to draw people to himself through these blessing encounters. We must have the conviction that God is always at work in the lives of people (even if they don't recognize it) and will continue to be. We have to believe God enough to put him on the line, trusting him to show up and show off in their lives. I think God is waiting on us to do just that!

## From Attractional to Incarnational

Traditionally, most churches have identified themselves as places where things happen and where congregants receive religious goods and services. As such, they produce worship services, programs, and events that attract people to attend. They provide club activities for club members who then rate the services they receive. In the members' view of church, it is something that exists apart from them; it's an organization, an institution. In this model, church is a place to frequent and to support by one's participation and gifts of time, money, and energy.

The scorecard for this kind of attractional church is attendance and participation, reflected in income it derives from satisfied customers. Since typical church members have spent their entire spiritual life in this system, it feels normal to them. Leadership for this model revolves around training people to operate this enterprise effectively. In many cases, the effectiveness of leaders relates to their ability to "grow" the church, meaning, of course, to improve its appeal and capacity to attract more people.

The incarnational understanding of who the church is declares that we are the body of Christ in the world today. Incarnational approaches focus on the church "being there"— at home, in the street, in the marketplace, at school, in the neighborhood—in the places where people live their lives. Incarnational believers search for ways to connect not just to each other but to the world beyond the church. They look for ways to help people discover and live out their faith in the spaces they already occupy.

A research scientist at a major university told me over lunch about his efforts to convene his colleagues around spiritual discussions in the research department where he works. "Not one of these people is going to go to church," he said. "Most of them are working on Sunday. If we don't find a way to be the church where they are, they will never experience it." In another city, a physician at a prestigious medical university moved to the worst part of town. His clinic is on the ground floor, and he lives on the two floors above it. Why? "How can I tell people that Jesus is there for them," he asked, "if I'm not willing to be there for them?" Sounds like a story we all know, doesn't it?

This is the spirit of the incarnational church.

Of course, not all expressions of attractional church are bad. It's a mistake to think so—and an instance of either-or thinking.

Even Jesus in his Incarnation was an attraction himself. The real issue is about DNA. The key lies in the motivation of the church. Does it see as its mission to grow, to compete for market share, to provide services? Is the Great Commission understood merely as a mandate to get more people to come to a church service or activity? If the answer to these questions is yes, then the DNA is attractional. On the other hand, is the fundamental motivation to carry on Jesus' mission in the world (beyond the church)? Is ministry guided by the idea that followers of Jesus *are* the church? Is helping them live intentional lives of blessing as they go about their daily routines the key strategy for partnering with God's mission in the world? Is the church celebrating the work of God in other spheres of activity other than church activities? If this is the case, the DNA is incarnational. In the former, more and better attractions are essential to achieve success. In the latter, the focus is on developing more intentional followers of Jesus.

One thing is certain: it is much more difficult to add incarnational DNA to an attractional culture than it is to incorporate attractional components into an incarnational approach. The attractional approach typically regards efforts that do not increase the bottom line as a loss, because the scorecard it is using has no way of celebrating such activities. The number of children attending Sunday school might be dwarfed by the number of students under the influence of the elementary school teachers who are a part of the congregation. Yet when it comes to assessing the church's "children's ministry," these teachers' work with children for dozens of hours a week doesn't make the scorecard; it is trumped by focusing on just a few hours of church activity. In fact, in an attractional church, many missionally engaged church members are rated low in commitment because they don't participate in many church activities. Those same public school teachers may even be devalued as church members because their schedules don't allow for them to accept committee assignments.

When I coach leaders who want to begin incarnational modes of church, I warn that if they begin with an attractional approach, the tail will always wag the dog. Since many people think church is the "gathering" aspect of church, I focus on how this needs to be approached. In the attractional model, worship easily becomes the show, perpetuating the unwarranted and mistaken notion that what happens when the church gathers represents the vitality of its mission. In reality, the gathering may just be the celebration of a few gifted people exercising their gifts while other people watch, a practice that has led to religious consumerism. The true vitality of a congregation rests in the abundant lives of its participants and in the blessed lives in the community it serves.

In the incarnational approach, attractional components point back to the mission in the world. The worship gathering, for instance, celebrates life beyond the gathering. Followers of Jesus gather to share tales of God's work in the world. They bring their stories of how God has shown up and shown off in their own life experience with others. These encounters are trophies of praise to God and expressions of encouragement to others who are on their own journeys of engagement with God and with the world. One congregation in the Pacific Northwest focuses purely on the stories of those who come, mostly from the arts community and many of whom are not yet Jesus followers. The pastor uses their stories to launch into spiritual themes, pointing to the God story behind each of their stories. Most of those present have never thought of God as working in their lives so proactively and are intrigued to pursue him.

The scorecard for the incarnational church has a much different metric than the level of participation at gatherings and church events. It ultimately measures its accomplishments by the quality of life of those in the faith community and the people they serve. The idea of being in competition with other churches is ludicrous. Incarnational believers are in competition with the kingdom of darkness that steals life from people.

If you are a leader in an attractional church mode and want to become more incarnational, you can do some key things to make this shift. Tell stories in sermons and on your Web site about life away from the church and how people bless others. Commission people as missionaries to apartment complexes, to business ventures, to school classrooms. One church even designated its executive pastor as a missionary to the local soccer culture when he became president of the league (a responsibility that took him away from church activities many Sundays but not away from the church's mission to bless people on their own turf).

Some other ideas include launching missional communities (more about this is coming up). Classes and small groups can be assigned to external ministries that target community needs such as tutoring kids in math. Make sure your musical groups have an external gig. It doesn't have to be a musical one. One church's contemporary worship team has a group ministry project of mentoring kids at the juvenile department of justice. You can adopt a school. We've spent so much time in the attractional church trying to get the community to connect to us; now we need to learn how to connect to the community. Whatever needs are prevalent in your community, the impact is showing up in your public schools. That's why adopting a school—asking how you can help—is the quickest way I know to become connected to the community beyond your church.

All these efforts to increase the ministry presence of the church beyond the church are good. They serve as important ways to help people practice being missional with their lives. However, if only corporate church efforts like these are celebrated, the point will be missed again. To become more incarnational, do everything you can to celebrate the life and ministry of people in their everyday lives beyond the church, right where they live, work, go to school, and have fun.

## From Member Culture to Missionary Culture

The attractional model of church creates a "member culture," in which people join a particular church and support that organization with their attendance, their money, their prayers, and their talent. The flow is toward the church, which is always at the center of the action, where the big game is being played.

The missional church is made up of missionaries, who are playing the big game every day. They live their lives with the idea that they are on a mission trip. On mission trips, people focus on the work of God around them, alert to the Spirit's prompting, usually serving people in very tangible ways, often in ways that involve some sacrifice or even discomfort. Life on mission is more intentional and more integrated. While the concerns of life (family, work, leisure) are pursued, they are part of a larger story being played out for the missionary. This story does not require a round-the-world excursion to discover or to pursue. Mission is not something "out there"; it is the defining quality of how missionary life is lived.

I meet followers of Jesus who are living a missionary life everywhere I go. Some work in health care, some teach in classrooms, others spend their days in research labs and doctors' offices, still others run sales routes, and some do hair and nails. These people are not wild-eyed fanatics unable to carry on normal conversations. They have families, face schedule stresses, and struggle to pay their bills. But they have that quality of "abundance" that comes only from living a life of an intentional blessing agent of the kingdom of God. A nurse I met in central California told me of her now twenty years of working with AIDS patients. She teared up as she recounted her opportunities to pray with them, share Jesus with them, help many reconcile to their families, and walk many of them into death. In all these years, she said, she is aware of only two of her patients who had not come into a personal relationship with Jesus. She wouldn't say this, but I will: they did that largely because of her ministry to them.

The member culture views society as a series of silos: politics, business, education, arts, media, technology, health care, social sector, and so forth. All of them are separate. The church culture has developed its own silo—a parallel culture in many respects—complete with schools, businesses, educational institutions, health care facilities, sports clubs, travel associations, and social agencies. Positioned as one silo among others, the church works to recruit people and resources from the other domains, vying for attention and money. In this way, the church effectively becomes a desalinization plant, sucking salt out of the community. Or a salt dome. Its activities serve effectively to take a lamp and put it under a bushel. The member-culture church violates the intent of God for his people by focusing its efforts on the spiritual silo.

The missional church views the church's position in society very differently. It understands that God has his people—his missionaries—deployed across all domains of culture. After all, since the mission is redemptive and the world is God's target, doesn't it make sense that he would take this approach? Otherwise, how would salt be distributed or light puncture the darkness? This deployment is what God has in mind when he designated his people to be a kingdom of priests (Exodus 19; 1 Peter 2; Revelation 4). This commission didn't anticipate a bunch of people tied up doing church work, insulated from the culture that needs priesting. God had a mission in mind that everyone could participate in, a far cry from a member culture that gathers on Sunday to watch a few people exercise their gifts.

Moving from a member to a missionary culture means making heroes of Jesus followers who are using their life assignments as missionary posts to bless people. The idea is that in their daily lives and daily routines, in their relationships and social networks, in their fields of influence, the people of God represent God to people and people to God. This is the work of priests. In a culture that doesn't know the gospel, it is the work of missionary-priests.

He calls it the "cigar bar church." Every Sunday night, Chuck gathers a group of guys together around cigars and some drinks. They talk about everything—everything. Including God. "These guys would never go to church," he says. "They'd shock everybody with their questions. Besides," he adds, "they don't let us smoke cigars in church." Chuck is no rabble-rouser; he's an ex-pastor who grew frustrated at not being able to reach men with his church programming. He's not alone in that track record—according to the 2008 Pew Forum Religious Landscape Survey, 19.6 percent of men in the United States have no religious affiliation whatsoever.[2] Chuck is providing a connection to the kingdom that doesn't come with all the church trappings that often obscure the primary point. Church is simple at the cigar bar: life is the issue; God is the conversation. Several of the cigar bar participants have become viral Jesus followers, infecting others with their newfound spiritual connections.

## From Proclamation to Demonstration

The modern church has assumed that the greatest need was to proclaim truth in a world increasingly hostile to God so that people could find their way to connect with him. Proclamation (preaching and Bible teaching) also helped keep the troops in line and pumped up. The result was and is a church culture that relies heavily on teaching to acquaint people with the ways and the work of God. Inevitably, since the lessons come from church documents, this approach has a built-in orientation to history or the past. We learn about God mostly from the witness he left us in the Bible and in his acts in history. In this system, clergy became authoritative voices telling us how the Bible should be interpreted, including doctrinal transmission and preservation.

The missional church recognizes a different dynamic at work. Missional Jesus followers believe that the way they demonstrate love and service will intrigue people to pursue getting to know the God who inspires such service. Using the life of

*But, how to educate?*

Jesus and the early years of the church as their reference point, they maintain that an authentic expression of faith requires Jesus followers to adopt an intentional life of blessing people. This, they believe, demonstrates the heart of God for people. Any and every follower of Jesus, not just a select few, can demonstrate God's love. It requires no special credentialing and so can result in the presence of Jesus around the clock, in every domain, wherever his followers live, work, and play.

Whenever I make the assertion that demonstration has eclipsed proclamation as the way of gaining a hearing for the gospel, some people think I am denigrating Bible study and preaching. I am not. People need biblical truth for living. Jesus followers hang on every word he said and is saying. This shift is about how people are engaged with the gospel in this culture and about shifting from an internal ministry focus (where preaching and teaching basically target believers) to an external focus that values the impact of the movement beyond church walls. Our acts of service and love, not our oratorical brilliance and institutional success, will intrigue people with our message. Jesus followers live the truth; they don't just study it. Because of this, others are invited into truth and life.

## From Institutional to Organic

The traditional church is and has been institutional for centuries. It focuses on its institutional goals, a church-year calendar, a place to belong, and a member culture. It is centralized in buildings and cared for by people hired to look after it. The staff of the institution develop and administrate its programs while attempting to meet constituents' service needs and expectations. In return, the members support the institution with the resources of prayer, time, money, energy, and talent. Church is just one part of life.

The organic church, in contrast, is decentralized, simple, not membership-driven, synched with normal life routines and patterns, not dependent on clergy, and focused on the spiritual development of the participants and the people they touch. "Supporting the church" is not an agenda item in the organic church expression. Nor is "attending church" or "going to church." This is because the people *are* the church. The church is not a thing that exists apart from them. Church is not a part of life for the missional follower of Jesus; it is the way of life.[3]

The move to organic will be possible only when and if leaders come to grips with a new way of seeing and understanding church. Nothing less than a total conversion from the institutional model will suffice. This process is painful and usually requires several touches for the miracle to work its way out (much like the two-step miracle of Jesus' curing of one blind man). The pain comes when the reality breaks through that much of what it takes to "do church" has very little to do with Jesus. The miracle occurs when the leader finds the courage to change the scorecard to reflect an incarnational church expression. This leadership shift is essential; that is why it is designated as one of the three major shifts required to engage the missional renaissance.

Once conversion from attractional to incarnational has occurred, leaders can begin to reshape the institutional culture by changing the conversation they have with the church. Storytelling and corporate celebrating will shift from focusing on church program activity and successes to celebrating the lives of missionary followers of Jesus in their efforts away from the institutional settings. One pastor making this journey has determined to interview people every week during his sermon to talk about their challenges and successes. Other communication venues shift as well. The Web site changes from being a bulletin board of church activities to a dynamic site sharing great stories of God's intervention in the lives of people through the intentional ministry of missionary-priests.

## From Reaching and Assimilating to Connecting and Deploying

The traditional church emphasizes "reaching" people through church "outreach" efforts and then assimilating them into the church. They generally involve an attractional component (an event of some sort that church people can invite people to, such as a concert). Most of the time, these events and emphases target the already convinced church consumer. Much of the church growth reported in recent years has resulted from the shopping and swapping of church members.

Once people are attracted to a church, they are assimilated through the process of socializing them into a community of faith, helping them feel a part of the congregation, and cultivating their sense of belonging. In the church growth days—where many church leaders still live—we knew that it took developing at least six significant relationships with people in the church within the first six months to help people "get involved" and "stick." The goal was to help the newbie feel that the church was their "home." Intriguingly, the upshot of this focus was that the socialization process was so effective that most churches could cut people off from their previous relationships within two years, replacing the old ties with a new "family." Of course, this hurt the church's chances of evangelizing along relational lines. How's that for mission?

The missional church, as you might guess, has an allergic reaction to the reach-and-assimilate social reengineering of people. The missional emphasis involves connecting with people where they live and deploying them as kingdom agents in their natural settings and established relational networks. The connecting and deployment modality also implies an agenda of connecting Jesus followers with each other to engage in an external focus by deploying to serve people in the community. Both aspects—connecting and deploying—help form the DNA of the missional church, distinguishing it from the church-centric approach.

Sherri engages with some fellow teachers in a "prayer and share" group. Twice a week during the school day, they meet to encourage one another and to figure out ways they can bless their school as followers of Jesus. "That group is my church," she told me during a break at a conference. The point of that group is to be connected to God, to each other, and to the world. They are already deployed in the mission field by virtue of their being on a school campus where they have influence and relationships. The typical church doesn't count this; in the missional church, this is what really counts.

## From Worship Services to Service as Worship

Worship in the attractional church has become another program offered for consumerist church people. Worship services are a primary way for churches to distinguish themselves from another in their tone and targeted constituency. Whether liturgical or nonliturgical, modern or postmodern, churches pay a lot of attention to style and production of the staple ingredients of music, teaching, prayer, offering, and announcements. Many times these worship services serve as thresholds for entry into the church.

Missional followers of Jesus have a much larger bandwidth for what they consider worship. Worship is not just what happens in corporate gatherings under the auspices and direction of people authorized to lead it. It has a much richer grounding in the biblical notion of worship as acts of honor in recognition of God's worthiness and in acts of obedience to him. The offering of obedience to bless others as the people of God is considered an act of worship. All of the missional communities I encounter set aside corporate days of service to their community as an act of worship. Many even use the traditional worship time in this way on a routine that frequently takes them away from their place of meeting into the community. Its frequency and rhythm match the life of the community. One congregation uses one Sunday per month as a day of service to the community. After congregants gather to pray and receive assignments, they head out to bless their town. Whole families will work together and often with other whole families during the day. Sometimes special challenges require an all-woman or all-teenager effort. The congregation then comes back together to share a meal and tell stories of encounters during the experience. At this church, service as worship replaces the traditional worship services every fourth Sunday.

People frequently ask me what worship looks like in an incarnational community. It is especially challenging for people steeped in attractional church to imagine something other than the Sunday event we call worship. The focus of the gathering in missional communities is primarily to celebrate the work of God in the life of the community, mainly through hearing stories of what God is doing right now in the lives of those present and in their relationships with others. Often a meal sets the stage for sharing these stories as well as hearing the needs of the group. Prayers are offered for healing and provision. Music is as varied as the group. Bible teaching, while practiced, is not the focus of the experience, as the sermon has become in most church services. Rather the central element is the sharing of God's immediate intervention and demonstration in the lives of those present. Worship is seen as the extension of normal routines, not something that is a discontinuity with the rest of the week.

Some missional communities may worship at some regional church on occasion or bring together multiple missional communities for a special occasion of worship. This practice is not unlike the rhythm and practice of the ancient Israelites, who mostly met locally and traveled several times a year to big "corporate" worship experiences built around the feast days.

For traditional congregations, practicing service as worship can serve as a key strategy for becoming externally focused. Many congregations around the country are beginning to set aside weekends for service. Robert Lewis, in *The Church of Irresistible Influence*, helped popularize this idea by recounting the story of Fellowship Bible Church in Little Rock, Arkansas.[4] Some communities, like Little Rock, are witnessing the rise of regional networks of churches who are cooperating in serving their communities.

## From Congregations to Missional Communities

For years, many of us have anticipated a new form of church life emerging as people begin to wake up to their identity as the people of God on mission with him in the world. Many in the church world have coached churches to become simpler, more streamlined, and intentionally missional. Some have predicted that the house church would find its way to America in a big way. Still others have suggested that postcongregationalist Christians would largely live out their faith through their day-to-day lives, not necessarily connected to any formal or organized expression of the faith.

This anticipated future has arrived in the form of missional communities in every culture where the Westernized Constantinian order is collapsing and the organic church is taking root.

Some examples can help you see what I mean. In Australia, one of my doctoral students oversees a network of missional communities in Sydney. These groups meet in pubs, in schools, in neighborhoods. They are basically groups of people doing life together and seeking ways to bless other people around them. They are covenantal and highly transformational, meaning that the participants are engaged with each other to encourage personal spiritual development and engaged with people around them as blessing agents Many participants have never been part of a traditional church or even considered themselves particularly religious.

Michael Frost, another Aussie and incarnational church thought leader, has chronicled his own journey into experiencing missional community.[5] The members of his community make five promises to each other in covenant: to be authentic, to serve a cause greater than themselves, to create community, to be generous and practice hospitality, and to work righteously as a way of being sent by God into the world. These promises are made to each other in the community; the proof is in their conduct of life beyond the community.

In Europe, what have variously been called "clusters" or "midsize groups" or "midsize mission" are the harbingers of the rise of missional communities there. A church planting initiative of Leadership Network has catalogued this development.[6] These clusters are larger than cells or small groups, most settling in between twenty and thirty participants. They build Christian community on days, at times, and in places that suit the group but are quite distinct from Sunday services. These clusters gain identity and purpose from a united mission vision that might be geographical or network-focused. They are also linked by a network of support and accountability to other midsize groups.[7]

Many of these communities adopt the Lifeshapes Triangle of UP-IN-OUT, first developed at Saint Thomas Crookes, in Sheffield, England.[8] UP signals relationship with God, as in worship. IN refers to relationship with each other, fellowship. OUT points to the relationship with those outside the group, the mission in the world. Rector Mike Breen made the discovery that groups focusing on IN and UP rarely get OUT. Groups starting with OUT and UP have little problems adding the IN dimension.

It's happening in America, too. A growing number of people are experimenting with some form of spiritual community that gives expression to their missional bent. From Neil Cole's LTGs (triads of disciples in covenant with each other for their growth) to some missional house church movements to more organized efforts like the Adullam community in Denver[9] and the dozens of contacts I get each month from people who are launching them. Some of these "planters" are theologically trained former church leaders. Others are business leaders who just want to make a difference in the world they encounter every day with people who will never "go to church."

The rise of these missional communities will be the green edge of the Christian movement in the decades ahead. They will emerge in every sector and domain of our culture. They will have all the characteristics of the internal-to-external shift discussed in this chapter. They will provide ways both out of and into the church. For some people for whom congregational life no longer provides a spiritual challenge, it will be a new way of expressing the followership of Jesus in the world today. For others, these missional communities will be the threshold for their entrance into the church as new Jesus followers. Some of these communities will organize around people's need to find others to "do life" with. Others will emerge around service projects as people discover others with similar passions. Some will develop around the affinity of neighborhood. Still others will flourish in workplace environments. Some will meet in "third places," while others meet in homes or marketplace locations.

My hope is that existing churches will see their way clear to expand the bandwidth of what they recognize as church to include these missional communities. Most congregations could sponsor dozens of these without ever harming their "bottom line" in terms of attendance and participation. These missional communities could, however, leverage an existing church's influence as salt and light across their community. They could energize and synergize the aspirations of people inside and outside the church to bring about huge societal impact. This will not happen, however, if these missional followers of Jesus are made to feel that they have "left the church." In fact, they are helping the church recover from amnesia about why it exists and for whom it exists.

## From There to Here

"I get it!" he exclaimed. John, a pastor and student in a doctoral course on missional leadership I was teaching, went on. "I have been thinking all along about changing the *church*. You are talking about changing the *world!*" I couldn't have said it better. He *did* get it. I literally saw the kingdom lenses flip into place. This is what happens when we engage the missional renaissance. Once we see what God is doing "out there" in the world, it changes everything we do "in here" in the church.

This chapter has catalogued a number shifts that churches and followers of Jesus must make in order to join the missional renaissance. Please keep several things in mind as you reflect on the enormous shift from internal to external. First, the shift is not suggested as an either-or scenario. Any group or movement has internal issues of logistics and maintenance, so an exclusive external focus is not even feasible. This shift is about a flow toward increasingly intentional efforts that help us realize what we are called to do and who we are called to be as the people of God.

Second, if you are giving leadership to the current church and feeling the pull toward missional, the descriptors offered in this chapter may help you explain the nature of the church and its mission to the people in your constellation of influence. Perhaps some of the descriptive shifts will help you diagnose your current situation and chart a course in the missional direction.

Third, in your personal life as a Jesus follower you need to determine whether or not your life is opened up to the world God wants to bless through you. Self-centeredness and self-absorption are tolerated, even encouraged, in the traditional church. This life stance is challenged by the missional perspective.

Finally, to make progress toward being externally focused, new behaviors will need to be implemented. Supporting these new behaviors will require a new scorecard that celebrates a new way of being and doing.

What could that scorecard look like? That's what we turn our attention to next.

# 4

## CHANGING THE SCORECARD FROM INTERNAL TO EXTERNAL FOCUS

"Something must be wrong with these numbers," my team leader said over the phone. He was reviewing potential church teams I was recruiting for a two-year leadership community convened around accelerating their missional journey. "This application says they only have an average weekend attendance of under fifty, but there's no way this list of community engagement could be supported by that few." I just chuckled. He would have been right if we were dealing with an internally focused program church. We weren't. We were dealing with a markedly different animal of the missional variety. The pastor has determined to bless the community where her congregation meets. She routinely involves several hundred more people per month in community service than attend her congregation's worship services on Sunday. Their efforts involve educational, political, and health care initiatives that require cross-domain collaboration.

This pastor is working off of a different scorecard than most congregational leaders. She embraces the missional shift to an external focus. She refuses to shrink-wrap her vision and passion to fit her small membership base. She is engaging the world beyond her church with the heart of Jesus for her inner-city neighborhood.

The missional church in North America needs to be measured in a completely different way from the metrics the traditional church has been using. Typically, results have been measured in church-centric and one-dimensional ways: how many (attendance), how often (volume of and participation in church activities), and how much (the offerings). This approach fails to capture the externally focused dimension of a missional expression of ministry. It assumes that church efforts and kingdom agenda are synonymous. Current scorekeeping actually keeps the church from going missional!

What gets rewarded gets done. This truth about human behavior shows up in every area of human activity: home, school, business, sports, you name it. It is true at church as well, because church people act like people everywhere. That is why scorecards being used to name and measure results are so important. They not only tell you how you are doing, but they also influence what you do in order to make progress or to win. That is why the current scorecard for most congregations actually militates against missional behavior. It rewards antimissional values; it promotes an antimissional ministry agenda.

Moreover, the scorecard issue is critical because it also determines how the performance of leaders and their churches is evaluated. So we have no option but to tackle the scorecard if we want everyone to be playing the same game. A shift in what counts and is counted does not happen automatically. It involves intentional and persistent effort and significant reeducation and modeling in your own life and ministry behaviors. But it all begins in knowing what that new scorecard should include.

So let's get started.

## Scorecard Categories: Refocusing Resources

We could take any number of approaches to creating a new scorecard for the missional church. One way would be to declare specific goals of ministry in terms of external accomplishments and then identify metrics to measure progress. For instance, a congregation may determine to help ministry constituents learn how to serve the community. One metric to check progress would be the number of people engaged in service; another would be the hours of community service rendered per month. This would be a significantly different scorecard than the typical approach of just tracking attendance at church events. A similar metric could be established on a per-project basis. This approach would be a good start. However, developing a multidimensional scorecard, celebrating both individual and corporate efforts, will require great sophistication.

To get you started thinking about these recalibrations, I have chosen a resource-based template for developing a scorecard. This approach focuses on both behaviors and outcomes. While you might look at the following pages of items as menu selections, please don't think the kitchen is limited to cooking up the kinds of things I've included! What you cook up will ultimately reflect your own missional appetites.

In a resource allocation model, we recognize that all spiritual leaders work with a common set of resources, regardless of their particular circumstances or challenges. These resources include prayer, people (leaders, others), calendar (time), finances, facilities, and technology. If leaders and organizations want to change their ministry scorecard, they have to reallocate or refocus these resources. We will take a look at each area, suggesting how resources in these categories might be refocused in the missional church. This reallocation will provide some ways that you might expand the traditional scorecard in each area by initiating or recording some different activities. If the notion of metrics and scorecards leaves you cold, try the notion of looking at what you currently celebrate and what you would celebrate in a move from an internal to an external focus in ministry.

## Prayer

Prayer may be the most untapped and underused resource available to the church for accomplishing its mission. Let's face it, most of the praying that goes on in many ministry organizations and congregations is spent on members and member activities. Imagine what would happen if the prayer scorecard shifted to supporting and reflecting an externally focused ministry agenda. Here are just a few ideas you might consider in recrafting your own prayer efforts to do just that. They are not offered in any order or priority but rather as a listing to prompt your further consideration.

## Prayer-Scaping

Jesus was once asked why he did what he did. His reply was, "I'm just doing what I see my Father doing." I frequently ask spiritual leaders what they are doing that they see God doing. Learning to see God, to hear him, is the real object of prayer. Its major objective is not to inform him or bend him to our purposes. The result of praying is to attenuate us to God's will and God's work going on all around us. If we ask God to show us what he sees, he will! And it will change us.

For example, each member of the staff at one church was instructed to go to a coffee shop, sit on a park bench, or stand in a mall parking lot and pray a simple prayer: "Lord, help me see what you see." They were to listen for an hour to the voice of God and then reconvene to share what they had heard. This simple outing radically changed their outlook as they realized that what was in the heart of God was much bigger than typical church concerns. They began to see broken families, homeless people, at-risk children, stressed teenagers—all people they were not engaging with their church ministry. Gripped by the heart of God, they gained an urgency to address what they saw.

The staff were so jazzed at what happened to them, they actually sent the church out on a Sunday morning to do the same exercise they had done. They then brought the congregation back later that day to discuss impressions. That church has never been the same. It has shifted from church-centric to kingdom-biased. The congregants are now working in several local schools, fulfilling the "wish list" needs of the district administration, providing tutors and paint and money and a bunch of other things as people turn up needs that they are eager to meet with the compassion of Jesus.

## Prayer-Walking

Congregations have engaged in prayer-walking for years. Prayer-walking can be done individually or as a group, in local neighborhoods or around some specific area that the Lord has asked the church to serve. Participants walk around certain blocks or set of blocks, praying as they go for the people, the businesses, the schools, whatever they see on their walk or are moved by the Spirit to pray for. Prayer-walking can be done as a churchwide effort at a given time or done by individuals at a time convenient for them. This activity serves to focus people's attention on what God is doing or wants to do in a particular geographical area. This is a wonderful ministry to encourage church members to engage in while walking in their neighborhoods for exercise. It is even more powerful if neighbors are aware that they can share issues and concerns with the prayer-walkers. Neighborhood prayer-walkers can drop notes in their neighbors' mailboxes or send e-mails informing each resident they are praying for the resident as they walk by the person's house. They can also invite neighbors to send requests to the walkers' e-mail or give them a call.

## Prayer Booths and Prayer Boxes

This involves some form of public prayer ministry that establishes a physical space where people can share their burdens and make prayer requests. One congregation encourages its members to put out prayer boxes at their workplaces where people can deposit prayer requests. Some congregations I have worked with actually set up booths at their county fairs or community festivals where people can drop off prayer requests and even be prayed for on the spot if they desire. Still other congregations take to the streets with roving prayer teams who engage people, asking if they would like to receive prayer. One denominational leader, hearing this idea, sent five hundred conferees into the streets of Chicago one afternoon just to be available to pray for people. The conferees would simply ask people, "Is there a special prayer I can pray for you today?" or "Is there some special way I can ask God to bless you today?"

## Adopting Community Leaders and Servants for Prayer

The idea here is to contact local community leaders, informing them that they have been adopted for prayer, and giving them some contact number for forwarding any prayer requests they might have. Sometimes it helps to prompt these leaders by telling them they can simply list the challenges they face and then assure them you will ask God to help them deal with these. It is important that the personal prayer champion's e-mail and phone number be given to that leader. Categories of leaders to include might be schoolteachers and administrators, governmental officials, police officers, firefighters, even sanitation workers! Public officials and public servants receive plenty of complaints. Imagine how encouraged they would be to receive news that there are people pulling for them!

## Praying for the Community in Worship Services

The challenges confronting our communities, from economic problems to social ills, need to be matters of prayer when we gather as Jesus followers. This gets the world beyond the church into the hearts of the people of God, since that world is definitely in God's heart. This practice of praying for the community can include the routine inclusion of a local leader, like the police chief or school superintendent, in the church gathering.

After interviewing these guests about the challenges they face, pray for them!

## Praying for Hospitality Staff in Restaurants

One church determined to pray for every waiter and waitress in town as congregants frequented local restaurants. Their simple question to these servers was, "In a moment, when I ask a blessing for my food, how can I ask God to bless you?" I personally practice this around the country and have had amazing conversations with many people who have jobs that never allow them to attend church in the traditional sense. In my wallet right now is the phone number and e-mail of a waiter I engaged in conversation just this week. He is a self-proclaimed "marginal theist" yet was eager to talk about spirituality. He volunteered his personal contact information just to make sure this happened.

## Community Prayer Meeting

We don't have to wait until another national calamity occurs to hold community meetings for the express purpose of praying for God's blessing on our town or city.

Many communities are beginning to hold multicongregational, citywide prayer meetings. These may be of any size, from small groups of pastors and church leaders to hundreds of people who gather merely to pray. Sometimes they are broken into groups with specific community needs to be prayed over. Sometimes they are led in a concert of prayer as someone guides the prayer of the participants from one issue to the next.

## Praying for the Lost

It is surprising how many churches rarely challenge people to pray for the salvation of people who need Jesus.

### Web Site Prayer

One obvious use of church Web sites is to ask people to e-mail prayer requests. The number of such requests can be tracked, especially the relationships that are established and prayers that are answered. People's identities will need to be protected, but anonymously posted requests and celebrations of prayer answers can be a powerful encouragement to people inside and outside the church.

### Coordinated Prayer

Through published prayer calendars, the church can coordinate and amplify corporate prayer efforts. Many congregations publish devotional guides during Advent. The same application can be taken at other times of the year, helping focus congregational prayer efforts to particular issues in the community.

### Prayer Request Feedback

One church includes a prayer request card in the food backpacks congregants fix for children in the public schools. The card contains an e-mail address and phone number that can be used to send prayer requests to the church. Another makes sure that every community leader can request God's help for the "impossible" items that cross their desks and agendas. Churches intentional in externally focused prayer efforts make sure they allow prayer requests to filter back from their external ministries—and then do something about it! They pray and often become God's answers to these prayers by their personal engagement.

## People

It is helpful to think of people as a ministry resource area in two parts: leaders, including staff and lay leaders, and all other people. This latter category can include people who participate in ministry as well as those who are the recipients of your ministry expressions.

The major thrust of the recrafting of this part of the scorecard is to shift from supporting a member culture to developing a missionary culture. A member culture focuses on church work, church real estate, church programming, and members' concerns. A missionary culture, on the other hand, focuses on the community and its needs, on ministry opportunities outside of the church.

Here are some possible steps to take toward the different behaviors required of an externally focused ministry.

## Leader Resources

• Include and develop community ministry responsibilities as part of every leadership role, particularly for staff members. These assignments should be based on passion and talent of the leader. Until church members see church leaders involved in this redeployment, they will not believe the external focus is critical. One congregation is well aware that its lead pastor serves as chaplain to the local police force.

• Some churches actually create a staff position to coordinate community development efforts. If you do this, just make sure that community engagement remains a part of everyone's responsibilities and doesn't get siloed into one person or position. That makes it too easy for staffers to assign all the community engagement to that person.

• Limit the number of church offices and roles that leaders can take on so that they have the essential time to be missionaries.

• Insist that every Sunday school class, small group, music ensemble, and ministry task force has some external community service component. These choices should arise out of the passions and interests of the groups. One class of senior adult women spends every Wednesday morning cleaning and taking care of babies at the home of parents who gave birth to quintuplets, adding five children to the two already present. These ladies clean, fold diapers, cook, and do whatever else needs doing, and they've made a pledge to do it until the children are old enough to go to school. Some groups will combine their efforts as they discover others who share their ministry callings.

• Bring community leaders into the church to educate your leaders on the needs of the community. This can be done during worship services and seminars, as well as through taped interviews and conference calls.

• Place staff leaders' offices in places other than the church. These can be strategically used to target certain populations or ministry possibilities. One church located its office complex in a mall where it could establish a ministry presence with merchants and special groups, especially teenagers. It also opened up a couple of rooms where kids could study or play games after school.

• Make staff leaders available to other organizations as a part of their responsibility. Your staff is capable of serving as mentors, coaches, advisers for microeconomic development, leadership training specialists, and tutors for all kinds of personal and family skill development. Maybe every staff member could be on assignment to a community organization like the Salvation Army or Big Brothers Big Sisters.

## Other People Resources

• Develop and publish a list of community needs, not just church jobs that need to be filled. These need to be prominent on church bulletin boards, in newsletters, in weekly worship folders, and on the church Web site.

- Establish and develop relationships and liaisons with community service agencies where volunteers who are willing to serve can be deployed.

- Keep track of volunteer hours, and publish them as an act of celebration of gifts and obedience.

- Count spiritual conversations and intentional acts of blessing. Part of every gathering should be the telling of stories of how God showed up and showed off this week through acts of blessing. These stories should also be posted on your Web site.

- Assign people to apartment complexes, trailer parks, and condominium communities to serve as resident missionaries. Then support them with volunteers, money, and whatever else is necessary as they uncover needs and minister to people. The percentage of people who leave group housing communities to attend church is minuscule. It doesn't matter if a church is next door or across the street. Putting boots on the ground is the best way to gain a presence in these high-density population areas. One church supports a young couple as its apartment missionaries, paying a stipend and meeting the needs that the missionaries uncover as they build relationships and ministry in their low-income apartment community. One Sunday school class prepares lunch one Saturday a month for the residents; another fixed up the complex's community room.

- Adopt a school. As was mentioned in Chapter Three, there is no more successful strategy than this to call out people and their talent for community ministry.

- Monitor the growth of the number of people engaged in some short-term ministry or missions project both globally and locally.

- Provide specific training for the skills people need in order to minister in the community. This might mean giving them tutoring skills for the school adoption initiative.

## Time and Calendar

An externally focused missional engagement will not work without a strong commitment of time and calendar to ensure that it is given high priority. Some ways to do that follow.

• Make time that staff and leaders spend in the community (including relationships with community leaders) a part of their performance measurement. Avoid the commonly held view that time spent in the community in ministry is an extracurricular activity. If that view prevails, it will ensure that community needs will be minimized compared to the other pressing needs of the church organization. The externally focused missional congregation has a very different view of community engagement. It is central, not a sideline.

• Make your church calendar a community calendar. If members feel that the church calendar is somehow different from the calendar of their community life, they will always feel that the community comes in second. By making sure that community events are calendared and not just church year stuff, you support your external focus. Be sure to have links on your page to major municipal Web sites, including chances to volunteer at significant places of ministry.

• Begin church planning with the community calendar. Typically, ministry planning at churches begins with the church calendar: "What did we do last January?" "When is homecoming?" and so on. Planning needs to begin with the community calendar—"When is the country fair?" "When do teachers go back to the classrooms?" "When does Shakespeare in the Park premier?"—if the church wants to have a significant presence at those community events.

• Reduce the number of church events on the calendar. The famed leadership expert Peter Drucker used to urge business leaders to practice "systematic abandonment" in order to stay lean and unencumbered with things that no longer produced results. Churches also need to do this in order to free up people's time to be missionaries in the community. The commitment to do this might just be the first sign of a true conversion to missional.

• Monitor the amount of time spent in worship where the community is on the agenda. This includes sermon time, prayer, sharing stories of blessing encounters, interviewing community leaders, all the things talked about in this chapter. Time spent on the community can also be measured in committee meeting prayer, planning for church presence at community events, and volunteer hours spent in ministry.

• Help church members see their existing community involvement, including the work they do for a living, as primary opportunities for ministry. You will do this by increasing the amount of time you spend celebrating people's everyday ministry in your gatherings. As one lay leader said at a conference, "This approach to ministry is so much simpler; I get to minister in the things I am doing already instead of just adding things to my to-do list."

• Develop a way for people to track their service hours each week; gather that information and use it to celebrate the increasing involvement of missional followers of Jesus in the lives of people around them.

## Facilities Resources

In a typical North American congregation, church facilities are constructed for the use of . . . guess who? Church members. And used for . . . guess what? Church activities and programs. We would never support such an approach by a missionary in another culture. In a missional church, the first question about facilities might be, "Do we really need to spend this money on buildings, or should we invest it instead in community infrastructure and need?" One church, considering the call to become missional, voted to remain in its current multiple school locations and to devote the millions of dollars collected to build a church building to key community initiatives instead. This accomplished two things: the church became a major investor in the community's health, and it kept its salt and light presence all over the city in the school locations. For this church, this was the appropriate response to God's call to be missionally engaged.

Not every church will make or needs to make the decision not to build. The question for those who do, however, shifts from "What are our building needs?" to "How can we build buildings to bless our community and then figure out a way for the church to use them?" One church, faced with having to tear down its old children's building because of environmental concerns, decided to build an after-school building for children and then figure out how church programming could fit in the space. This approach reflects the missionary heart. We expect missionaries in foreign countries to do this. If a town or village needs a well, we expect missionaries to dig a well; if health care is needed, we expect a clinic to be constructed. North America is the largest English-speaking mission field in the world. We can no longer think and act like club members; we must think and act like missionaries.

Another question for churches with facilities is, "How can we use what we already have to bless the community?" The typical church has thick policy manuals aimed at keeping the community out of its buildings. The missional church figures out ways to serve the community with the facilities it has.

Following are a few scorecard considerations to reflect the shift to an externally focused perspective on church facilities.

• Get educated on community facility needs that might intersect with your facility capacity. Does Big Brothers Big Sisters need a place to stage its work? Do AA groups need places to meet? Does the local food bank need another distribution point or a location for a Kids Cafe? One church discovered it could both serve hot evening meals to kids who didn't have enough to eat and offer seminars to parents in basic life skills, once it opened up its fellowship hall to being used for more than feeding club members at church activities. Another church has turned its indoor basketball facilities into a major community gathering place by working with the local department of recreation. By the way, prayer boxes are prominent throughout the facility, and routine announcements are made about the availability of people to pray with people and offer counseling.

• Partner with schools to provide meeting space, training space for teachers, space for concerts, after-school computer labs, and so on.

• Allow other churches to use your facilities for their own community efforts.

• Consider land use. One congregation owned a lot of property on which building development was prohibited. For years, it had merely been green space until the church realized it could be used as the "neighborhood's backyard." This vision led to all kinds of creative uses of their space, including creating an outdoor movie venue. Another church decided that its first construction effort was going to be sports facilities, since it owned more than 30 acres of land adjacent to new housing developments that had green space but no recreational areas.

• Look for offsite facilities that could serve as ministry venues for missional engagement in the community. You might need to buy that abandoned restaurant in a declining neighborhood that you can turn into a great soup kitchen and after-school program place. You might want to lease space in a mall to create an alternative hangout spot for teenagers. Consider beginning missional communities in gated communities' club spaces and lawyers' offices conference rooms.

• Along with small group and worship attendance, why not track and report how many people used your facilities each week for AA meetings, food collection, mentoring, and other activities as a way of measuring how well you are allocating facilities resources in a missional way?

• Create uses in your current facilities that bless the community in entrepreneurial ways—think coffee shops, art galleries for local artists, concert venues for local musicians, incubator spaces for young businesses. In other words, don't limit your thinking to ministry to the underserved portions of the community; consider the advantaged as well.

• Make sure your facilities say "You are welcome here" in every possible way: signage, easy accessibility for handicapped persons, listing of community events, good parking lot lighting, adequate and clean restrooms, and so on.

## Financial Resources

The clearest sign that a conversion from "churchianity" (internally focused and church-centric) to missional engagement has occurred shows up in the church budget. Of the roughly $300 billion North Americans give each year to charity, about one-third goes to religious charities, including local congregations. The stewardship of these vast resources weighs heavily on spiritual leaders in light of the huge needs evident in our culture. Consuming these monies for our own benefit, with no community transformation to show for it, is an indictment of those who claim to follow the One who promised that he came to give abundant life to all people.

The missional church not only allocates resources to different things than the typical church but also develops revenue streams outside what is collected from the people in the pews. Here are a few suggestions.

- First of all, make sure that more dollars and a greater percentage of revenue go toward community ministry investment than toward internal expenses. One congregation budgets $2 for external ministry for every $1 spent on its facilities.

- Develop and conduct a community ministries capital drive just as you've done for facilities construction in the past. One pastor's first building campaign was to raise over $100,000 in pledges to jump-start three community ministry initiatives targeting homelessness, hunger, and AIDS.

- Add a community component to any capital stewardship drive you conduct. One church tithed its capital campaign results to the local food bank. This does a couple of things. First, it signals that the church's focus on buildings does not trump a focus on people. Second, people will actually give more money if they have options to designate their monies to ministry ideas that excite them. Furthermore, this is a very powerful combination if the church is following the externally focused use of buildings as an operating principle, so that money used to build buildings is regarded as a community investment rather than a church investment.

- Partner with businesses. Many corporations set as part of their business plan a quota of money they must spend on local community projects. Why not capitalize (pun intended) on this? Their money might just fund some of your ideas. At the same time, your volunteer base might enable them to consider larger projects than they can address with limited personnel. Businesses might build your playgrounds and outfit your computer labs if they are community-oriented. And don't limit your thinking to kids and the poor here; think senior adults, for example.

- Write grants. Your church already has grant writers if you have schoolteachers or administrators. You can also hire grant writers, either outright or for a percentage of the money they generate, to discover streams of income for you from faith-based government initiatives, family foundations, and business funds. A new metric of this externally based scorecard has to do with the number of grants received as well as the dollar amount. One woman I met carries on a ministry to street kids by garnering over $100,000 annually in government grants. Her goal is to send these kids to college. Her first graduate earned his college degree in 2007.

• Establish one or more 501(c)(3) nonprofit organizations targeting community ministry opportunities. Many businesses and foundations are free to contribute to financial entities other than churches.

• Invite community leaders into your budgeting process. Let them inform you of needs and possible sources of revenue.

• Create a foundation that can receive bequests and manage investments for long-term income stream development. Some churches are beginning to set up development offices (as universities have done) to capture some of the trillions of dollars of wealth becoming available as money accumulated by senior generations is being left behind. Many churches have never even explored this with their own church members by way of personal and family financial planning.

• Offer financial planning seminars and services to the community, especially to help less affluent members of the community know how to budget better and plan for the future.

• Partner with other congregations. In the traditional church, congregations competed against one another for dollars. In the missional church world, the problems being addressed are too big for one person or group to tackle, raising the need for cooperation between congregations.

• Pursue microeconomic developments to help people start their own businesses or participate in the economy. One group of churches is creating jobs in the hospitality sector by buying hotels and operating them—in a foreign country. We need to do more here in North America of what we have been doing overseas. This can have a huge impact in urban areas particularly. Some of the funding can come from corporations and foundations. The human capital can come from your pews.

• Create your own venture capital funds as part of your church budgeting. Then take applications for grants and loans from people who have ideas on how to use the money to improve community service.

• Find ways to help members monitor their own consumption expenses and reduce them. Celebrate freeing up monies for ministry personally and corporately by keeping track of how much money has been saved and redirected. Note that this will have to be modeled at the leader level, or it will not gain any traction among members.

• Develop ways for members to contribute to community causes through the church. Encourage this rather than seeing it as a threat to "church money." One church created a special account to receive monies to build a $28,000 playground for a poor neighborhood. The goal is to create generous people, not just make the church a recipient of generous people.

• Come up with clever ways of giving to the community. One church makes it a point to give to the community money at least equal to the property taxes it would pay if it had to pay those taxes. It works with local government agencies to figure out the apportionment to various government services.

## Technology Resources

In the church-centric world, technology supported ministry. In the missional world, technology creates ministry and ministry venues while supporting other resources and efforts.

Technological applications will help most of the resource refocusing I have already mentioned. Here are just a few ways you can enhance your move toward greater missional engagement.

• Make sure your Web site enables people to access prayer concerns and report on prayer answers, sign up for community projects, and share ways that God has shown up and shown off in their encounters when blessing people, access community needs, make online donations for ongoing as well as emergency needs, take online training sessions in dealing with "frequently asked questions" regarding the faith, and become aware of partnering organizations who share passions similar to theirs.

• Take advantage of the social spaces on the Internet, such as Facebook, MySpace, and YouTube, to connect people for ministry and for sharing of stories.

• Create podcast interviews with community leaders for updates on what's going on in your location.

• Become an incubator for local volunteerism by posting community needs on your Web site, allowing people to sign up to help with projects or donate money, and providing links to other local agencies' Web sites.

• Measure "hits" on your various ministry offerings to determine interest and where resources need to flow.

• Conduct community forums or "Webinars" to educate people to missional opportunities.

• Explore and use cell-phone technology (texting, for instance) to update people and remind them of ministry opportunities. Student ministries already use broadcast text-messaging to connect with students during the week.

• Blog your missional engagement as a way to spread the missional virus.

- Create visual graphics that show needs, demographic trends, and member engagements in community.

- Gauge the number of nonmember interactions with your Web site.

- Publish weekly or monthly video announcements featuring community needs and service projects and opportunities.

- Post celebrations and commentaries on various service projects on your Web site.

- Create engaging gospel presentations online; allow for response and follow-up. Use videos as well as text.

The missional church scorecard has a much wider bandwidth than the current scorecard in place for the North American church. You can help create it as you do the hard work of taking the ideas mentioned here, plus your own, and figuring out the appropriate metrics that signal accomplishment in each area.

Your scorecard for your congregation or ministry should reflect your own vision and values. It needs to support what you are trying to accomplish and how you are going about getting it done. Developing the right scorecard will help establish the accountability that will turn your dreams into reality. It will also give you opportunities to celebrate progress made on your journey into the missional renaissance. A better world will be the ultimate result of your efforts.

# 5

# MISSIONAL SHIFT 2: FROM PROGRAM DEVELOPMENT TO PEOPLE DEVELOPMENT

I remember it as if it were yesterday, even though it was over twenty years ago. We had just completed a midweek leader luncheon at the two-year-old church where I served as founding pastor. Everyone else had left the building. I sat alone in the fellowship hall. And the Lord spoke to me. It was in the form of a question: "Are people better off for being a part of this church, or are they just tireder and poorer?" As a young church, we were spending massive energy in our ministry effort, adding staff, raising money to build our first permanent facility on our 24-acre site.

The question bothered me. A lot. Not only did I not know the answer, I feared knowing! I realized that I had no way of gauging people's personal growth; I only had ways to measure their church involvement. I knew how often they came to church activities, but I had no idea how often they served their neighbor. I tracked weekly worship attendance, but had no real sense of how many marriages were healthy and growing. Bottom line: I could tell how busy people were with church but not how their lives were going.

The harsh awakening resulting from that encounter changed our ministry focus as a church. We shifted our schedule, our programming, and our content of ministry to be more intentional about developing people. Our efforts were sometimes clumsy, and they were not universally embraced by members of the congregation who were used to the show. But even back then, the seeds of this missional shift, the move from program to people as the focus of the community of faith, were being planted in my thinking. And I'm even more convinced now of the need to focus on people's development.

I must warn you that this second missional shift is very difficult to address. First, it's hard for those of us steeped in the program church even to get our minds around what this shift means. Second, this shift so dramatically changes the scorecard that it threatens those of us who lead the program church. We know how to produce and to execute programs. Developing people? That's a different animal. We have operated off the faulty assumption that if people participate in our church programs, they will grow and develop personally. In reality, that may or may not be true. Finally, this shift is a challenge because it moves us to a place where our work is never done. We can check off our fall program calendar week by week as events occur, but people just don't ever seem to get "done."

We are so good at programming, we can deceive ourselves with the false notion that we can program missional into the church. If we aren't careful, we can even turn the first missional shift, the move from an internal to an external focus of ministry, into a new program of community involvement. In fact, if we just get the first missional shift without appropriating this one, two things will happen. First, we will wind up wearing everyone out in the church with a new program of community service, just as we are doing with our current ones. Maybe even faster! Second, we will fail to use the ministry touches with people as part of a development strategy for them. Developing people requires building relationships, not just delivering a product or service. Absent a real commitment to actually helping people grow, the ramp-up of services will not fully convey the heart of God to people who need to experience it.

I don't want you to pass over this last observation hastily. Let me reiterate that this second missional shift affects people inside and beyond the church. We should feed hungry people. But when their stomachs are full, we should also teach them or mentor them or find them work, whatever we can do to elevate their capacity to provide for themselves. This moves them from being mere charity cases to being people. This turns our external ministry from being just another program of engaging church people in activity into engaging them with people as God's partner in his redemptive mission. God is not more interested in developing people inside the church than those outside it.

Throughout this chapter, however, most of my comments about people development target the church culture. This is true for a couple of reasons. First, since I am speaking to a number of congregational leaders in traditional church settings, I want to point out the revolutionary shifts necessary to foster an environment favoring the growth of people. More important, there is no missional church without missional followers of Jesus. We do not share the heart of God with the world because we do not have the heart of God. This heart transplant does not occur by participation in church activities. It comes from being in a vibrant, growing relationship with God. We can do better than we have done. Simply put, the church in North America has focused on developing programs, not developing people. It is time for this to change.

## The Rise (and Fall) of the Program-Driven Church

We have not always been a program-driven church. I spoke some years ago at a church that didn't meet every week for the first hundred and fifty years of its existence. It met every other week, only for worship and dinner on the grounds. No program church could do that today—everyone's too desperate for the revenue! Besides, who would join a church that doesn't offer a full-service menu?

There was a time when churches did not operate everything from child care to retirement homes. The church calendar used not to have entries for every day of the week. Churches used not to have staff program coordinators for every age group, much less full-time development officers to seek your support even after you die!

I maintain that the rise of the program-driven church correlates directly with the rise of the service economy in post–World War II America. The manufacturing engine powering the economy yielded to the service sector as Americans could afford to pay other people to do things they no longer wanted to do themselves or couldn't do themselves. People began to outsource food preparation, lawn maintenance, laundry, oil changes, and child care. And Americans outsourced spiritual formation to the church. It was during this period that the concept of church as a vendor of religious goods and services became entrenched in the ethos of the North American church culture.

The demanding service expectation on the part of church families drove the church to proliferate its offerings in children's and student ministries at first. This was followed by scores of other programs in an increasingly market-driven approach to capturing church members. The church growth movement of the last quarter of the twentieth century fed this frenzy as churches clamored for customers who could support the program expansion. The result was a resettling of the church population into congregations who have both paid attention to this program expectation and fed it as well.

Church programming became increasingly complex as churches became more adept and more able to develop ministry options. The assumption grew that the church could provide the venues and opportunities for people to live out their entire spiritual journey as part of a church-sponsored or church-operated activity. This approach to Christian life has gone on now for so long that it seems natural and normal to North American church people. In fact, some of you reading this don't see this as a problem for the mission of the church.

"Isn't the church supposed to be the center of a person's spiritual experience?" you might be wondering if you are a product of this era. No, it's not. Everyday living is where spiritual development is worked out. The program-driven church has created an artificial environment divorced from the rhythms and realities of normal life. Its claims that participation in its consuming activities will result in spiritual growth is preposterous. It cannot deliver on this promise, because the premise is false. Loving God and loving our neighbors cannot be fulfilled at church. Being salt and light can not be experienced in a faith huddle. Engaging the kingdom of darkness requires storming it, not habitually retreating into a refuge.

We were told that if we built successful churches, people would come. We bought and paid for the lie that Six Flags over Jesus was what the world needed. We believed that if we built better churches, our cities would be better off. We telegraphed in dozens of ways the message that involvement in church life was the portal to fulfillment and the mark of an abundant life.

The jig is up! Evidence of this is everywhere and growing, both outside and inside the church culture. The program-driven church has produced a brand of Christianity that is despised, not just ignored, by people outside the church. Their antipathy for what we call Christianity exists for all the wrong reasons.[1] Basically, it comes down to our failure to demonstrate the love of Jesus, passing by people not like us on the other side of the road on our way to building great churches.

Even among the self-defined committed, the evidence is clear that church activity is no sign of genuine spiritual vitality. The lifestyles and values of church members largely reflect those of the culture. A gnawing unease among church members about their own lack of personal growth has erupted into a growing disaffection and disillusionment with the church's program approach. The widely touted *Reveal* study by Willow Creek has outed the problem for all to see.[2] In that internal study, Willow discovered that its most engaged members were expressing significant frustration with their own personal growth. In fact, many were contemplating leaving the church! If this flagship program-driven church can't deliver, there's not much hope for those following in its wake.

The eclipse of the program-driven church does not mean the demise of church programs, nor does it mean that programs are bad in and of themselves. Often people leap to that assumption when they hear me talking about this shift. This shift just calls for a clarification of the role of programs in the development of people and the adoption of a new scorecard built around people's successes, not program successes. The key idea is moving away from a *program-driven* church culture, meaning that the church takes its measure from the quality of its programs rather than the quality of its people.

Nor should one assume that this shift is a slam on megachurches. For one thing, megachurches aren't the only churches that are program-driven. Some of the most rigid organizations in the world are small congregations that are purely programmatic. I passed a small church building in upstate New York that had its worship times chiseled in granite on its sign out front! Many megachurches are quite willing to undertake this shift toward people development. For one thing, they are tired of doing what it takes just to keep the beast fed. As one weary staff member of a megachurch said to me recently, "We have to keep coming up with something new all the time." In addition, megachurches are able to customize their constituents' spiritual journey because the number of programs in their portfolio enables them to create diverse interfaces with people.

## Fostering a People Development Culture

Fostering a people development culture requires some distinct shifts in our thinking and behavior. The following characterizations can help you move in this direction. Taken separately, these directional moves do not accomplish this second shift of the missional renaissance. However, together they can serve to help give you language to talk about the changes you want to make. They may help you knock the fuzzies off your own thinking as well as give you a way to communicate these insights with the people in your ministry constellation.

## From Standardization to Customization

The program-driven church came of age as the ultimate expression of the modern world's ability to achieve mass standardization. The technologies undergirding the modern era made possible the mass delivery of standardized components that were identical, from car parts to contact lenses. When applied to the church world, the technology of mass customization meant among other things the development of a widespread uniformity of expectations of what church would look like. This dynamic supported denominations and teaching-church efforts in establishing their brand identity, allowing the franchising of programs to establish and maintain tribal distinctions. A Baptist Mac tasted like a Baptist Mac everywhere. The rise of the megachurch culture was driven in part by the capacity to create associations linked to teaching churches whose methods and programs could be replicated. It was a plug-and-play world, supported by a mass standardization mind-set and delivery system.

Standardized approaches treated people as market segments by age, gender, and life circumstance (college student, single or married, and so on). This allowed program development to target groups with increasing sophistication. This process took on a life of its own. It wasn't long before the need to maintain these programs reversed the relationship between people and programs. People, once considered beneficiaries of program delivery, now became resources (possessors of time, talent, and money) to feed the programs. Initially developed as supportive to people's lives, programs now placed demands on people. Only a program-driven church could conceive of something like a Sunday school growth campaign, as though this organization were a living thing! Only in a program-driven culture could spiritual leaders convene and ask each other, "How's your church doing?" (referring to its program health) as opposed to "How are your people doing?" The program-driven church became identified by its distinctive programs.

The mass standardization of the modern era has given way to mass customization of the postmodern world. Once again, this development has been made possible by technological breakthroughs, particularly the digital revolution. You can customize your new car or build a computer by selecting its features online, customize your coffee at Starbucks, select your ringtones on your customized cell phone, create your own playlist on your iPod, and record your favorite TV shows on your DVR so that you can watch them when it's convenient for you.

Can you even imagine a world where you had to select from only the cars in stock, buy computers off the shelf, figure out when lattes were being served, have to purchase an entire CD to get one song you really want and then sit in front of fixed speakers to hear it, and arrange your life to accommodate the TV broadcast schedule so you can watch your favorite show? No way! That world would be archaic, like the 1980s.

It would be kind of like trying to fit your life into the program church. Or trying to imagine that your life rhythms and developmental preferences would match the schedule and options of church programming. Truth is, for anyone not already accustomed to this culture, it just doesn't have an appeal or even make sense. Bible study available for one hour a week, Sundays only? With a group of people that someone else chose for you? Worship confined to a corporate schedule put together by people who don't have Sunday jobs (except at church)? And why is it again that I have to wait till September to form a small group or gain permission from a church leader to involve a nonchurch person in a ministry effort to the homeless? And participate in only one church's ministry? Weird, huh? But it feels normal to many of us who have spent our entire lives in it.

People are no longer going to let the church or church leaders provide the template for their spiritual journeys. Postmoderns do not know why they should have to search for God on church time and church real estate. Nor do people automatically believe that other people know what's best for them or that one organization can meet all their spiritual needs.

On the one hand, this really is bad news for the program-driven church. It means that the bandwidth of the population at large that fits its program configuration is limited, maybe even shrinking. On the other hand, this news opens up exciting possibilities for leaders and congregations who are willing to rethink their approach to ministry.

People often ask me, "Doesn't this customization feed the consumer church economy?" The answer would be yes if we were trying to sell a product (which the program-driven church often is). But the "product" and "purchase" we are after in this case is a Jesus follower who is more convinced and more intentional than ever to pursue the life Jesus wants for the person. That's hardly a consumerist outcome!

## From Scripting to Shaping

For centuries, clergy leaders told people how they should grow spiritually—attend services, discover their gifts, get involved in a small group, run the base paths, whatever. And people did it, for several reasons. One was a then-prevailing worldview that allowed for authoritative hierarchies. Another was a restriction of information so that spiritual insight was disproportionately owned by those with theological degrees and specialized training. All this has changed. Just as people are taking greater roles in choosing their educational pursuits, designing their workplaces, and managing their health care, they feel increasingly qualified to craft their own spiritual quests.

However, the fact that people are no longer willing to let others, including and especially the church, script their spiritual journey doesn't mean that they are unwilling to be coached. People will accept help in shaping their spiritual path. In fact, they welcome it, especially from people they respect and trust, who seem to have their best interests at heart.

Some years ago, I joined a YMCA near my home. I met with Jason, the resident trainer who worked out of a glass cubicle in the room of torture. What if, when I went to see Jason, he had challenged me to prove my commitment to the Y by getting on all those machines in the room? Further, suppose he had pulled down a picture of Mr. Universe to show me my goals and predetermined regimen. Would this have seemed strange? Of course it would have! But that's what would have happened if the YMCA operated like the program-driven church. (Actually, if the Y operated like the church, it'd bring people in once a week, feed them coffee and donuts, and let them watch Jason work out!)

What Jason actually did was ask me a simple question: "What would you like to accomplish at the Y?" Based on my response, he customized for me a path through that room. He didn't let his training overpower me. I'm sure one quick look at me had him thinking of several things I should have wanted to accomplish on those machines. But he didn't lecture me on what I needed to do. Because he invited me into the discussion, he earned my trust and made me more receptive to his advice.

Spiritual leaders, pay attention! Of course we know what people should do with their lives. After all, God has told us to tell them, and we get paid to do it. But what if we actually begin to see ourselves as responsible for creating a culture where people get to participate in customizing their spiritual journeys based on their spiritual appetites and ambitions?

We as clergy leaders were trained for the scripting role. We've got a lot to learn for the coaching role. We were trained primarily to talk, not to listen, but listening is a very important aspect in gaining access to people's hearts. You know the difference when a teacher or a doctor or a restaurant manager or a car technician dials in and listens to you. The hunger for this is just as profound in the spiritual aspects of life. When it comes to offering spiritual direction, the person we are engaging actually matters. We start with the other person's problems, dreams, needs, and receptivity and then work to shape an individualized path toward personal development and maturation.

"Wait a minute!" I can hear you saying. "This is very labor-intensive! I don't have time to do this and manage all the stuff I take care of." You are right on both counts. It is much harder to do what I'm talking about than to develop a template and then force people into it. And what does it say about us that we in spiritual leadership are too busy for people? Do I recall some parable about that involving a Samaritan?

You don't have to abandon all your fine programs to pursue engagement with people's spiritual journeys. You will likely even use available programs when creating a portfolio of activities designed to accomplish each pilgrim's quest. It's all a matter of beginning point and perspective. In the program-driven church, you begin with programs and look for people to make them happen. In a people development–driven culture, you begin with people and then use established programs or whatever else it takes to help them grow.

I can give you a couple of concrete examples of what I am talking about. A church I am working with right now has decided to pursue this missional shift with great intensity. It has invited its members to participate in interviews designed to explore their spiritual quests. Conducted by the pastors and other senior church leaders, these conversations are engaging people in answering specific questions about what they would like to see God do in their lives. Based on their responses, the leaders are coaching them into some activities and programs that will help them achieve their spiritual goals. Another congregation is creating online spiritual and life coaching, offering people suggestions of specific resources to consult and church programs to participate in that specifically target their stated life objectives and spiritual needs. These efforts put programs in their proper place—as a resource to help make people successful.

## From Participation to Maturation

In the program-driven church, we track participation. Who comes to church? How often? Do they participate in small groups or fellowship functions? Do they participate in funding drives and regular offerings? These participation items tell us how "involved" they are in the "life" of the church—meaning its programs.

In a people development culture, the key issue is maturation. Are people growing in every aspect of their life? Are they becoming more like Jesus? Are they blessing the world as the people of God?

There is no necessary correlation between time logged sitting in pews and attaining godliness. Unfortunately, I've got plenty of evidence to back up this observation. I have negotiated severance packages for good pastors persecuted by club members who never miss a Sunday. I have run into racism staunchly defended by very dedicated church members. Conversely, I have encountered the Spirit of Jesus profoundly demonstrated in people who never pass through the doors of a church. Those in this latter group cannot possibly be "good Christians" according to the church participation scorecard.

Maturation is messy. It takes time. It doesn't occur linearly. Maturation occurs in an atmosphere where accountability is expected and practiced. In this environment, people are coached, challenged, and celebrated in their journeys. Remember Peter's journey in the New Testament? The reason we so easily identify with him is because our life experience often resembles his. One minute, we are champions of the faith, coupling brilliant insight with passionate devotion. The next, we are cowed by those around us. But Peter was a part of a spiritual community that kept pulling him forward.

## From Delivering to Debriefing

The program-driven church often focuses on teaching, in an autocratic manner, especially for adults. The delivery of a Bible lesson or a sermon occupies a large part of the agenda, both in worship and in religious education venues. Those who carry the responsibility for this teaching tend to think their job is accomplished when they deliver their goods, defined as the teaching or information. Their effectiveness is generally rated on their delivery prowess, not on the level or scope of transformed living among their listeners. This approach fails to reckon with how people develop. The only performances that count are those given by the official deliverers. People are then left with the job of applying what they have "learned" in these contexts.

The truth is that people need help debriefing their lives. They need to examine their experiences to learn from them. The goal of debriefing is to help people make sense of what is going on in them and around them. In earlier times, people accomplished this while lingering over meals with their family and engaging in late-night discussions on front porches or on the phone with friends in extended conversations. In that world, we could operate a church agenda focused on merely providing information for those discussions. Now we have to *stimulate* those discussions for people because they aren't making time for them anymore, due to the frenzied pace and isolation of contemporary life.

Let me explain what I mean with a metaphor. I am an asthmatic. The problem with asthma is very specific. I have trouble breathing out. This means that old air gets trapped inside my lungs. When you have lungs full of old deoxygenated air, you can't suck in fresh oxygen-rich air. An asthmatic can suffocate in a room full of oxygen. You can choose to treat asthma sufferers by pumping oxygen into the room (which really won't help) or administer medications that allows the asthmatic to expel air. That does the trick.

Every week, people come into our churches with old air trapped inside of them. This is their life experience, what's happening in their lives. The program-driven church has spent its efforts titrating the oxygen levels in the room (making sure the worship is stellar, the sermon is prepared and delivered well, the programs go off without a hitch). But unless we help people exhale, they can't take in all this rich stuff. What they need is help in breathing out—in debriefing.

Intentional debriefing should be part of our routine gatherings, whether in worship experiences or in small group encounters. You may have to fight your physical and programmatic architecture to pull this off. People lined up in pews have to be given specific permission and instruction ("Turn around and tell someone close to you the best thing that happened to you this week"). People in classroom settings need help moving past simple chitchat (as important as that is in creating emotional connections) or discussion about the curriculum to specific encounters designed to help them unpack their lives. You can come up with a revolving question of the week to do this. "What was the biggest challenge you faced this week?" or "What worries you most these days?" or "What about this past week is a cause for celebration?"

Life debriefing requires an environment that is very differently shaped than the one crafted to focus on the delivery of information. One of the dilemmas of the program-driven church experience is the often frenetic pace of its activity. People race from one activity to the next. This squeezes out all the white space in people's time together, space that is crucial in order to allow for genuine conversations. This means that we have to be even more intentional to create pockets of white space even inside our activities for people to connect for this all-important function of getting help in debriefing their lives.

Let me give you just a couple of examples of what I am talking about. After we preach a sermon, we should ask people to declare to one or two people seated around them what they will take away from the message. Or perhaps we ask them to state one or two things they will do with what they've just heard or one or two things they will do differently based on the truth that has just been shared with them. The same thing should happen in every Bible study class or small group. I am afraid that for years, I helped people learn how to resist the Spirit! How? Not intentionally, of course. I did it by not letting them declare anything about what they were going to do with the truth. As a result, I helped them develop immunity to being accountable with what God was showing them. They could "amen" with their heads and plan not to do a thing differently with their hearts or their hands. This means, of course, that I would have had to teach and preach with the idea of actually generating a desire to do something differently or to be different!

Routine debriefing can also enhance the life-transformational capacity of our community and service engagements. When people perform a day of community service or participate in an overseas mission excursion, we should debrief them afterward. Questions could include "What did you learn? About people? About God? About yourself? Did you find prejudices or biases you have that were challenged? What part of this experience or insights from this experience can you transfer into the rest of your life? How will your life be different from this experience?"

The practice of life debriefing will also have the spiritual benefit of helping people see that God is active in their lives every day in every sphere. This is fundamental to helping people live more intentional and more missional lives.

## From Didactic to Behavioral

The focus on helping people debrief their lives, especially toward the overall objective of helping them grow, challenges the current program-driven church's bias toward didactic environments. The didactic approach is teacher-dominated and information-focused, usually curriculum-driven. While there are times and places where this is appropriate, an entire system constructed around this perspective fails to deliver on its promises. It turns out well-informed people who can be adept at avoiding key issues in their personal development. Giving people information without providing means for application and accountability for their behaviors turn them into knowledgeable but disobedient people.

The program-driven system favors a culture that creates church customers, not followers of Jesus. It makes people who can spout off all the right answers but live unaccountable to the truth. The missional church, by contrast, dares to move into the arena of life development by meddling with people's behaviors. After all, this is the crux of the matter when it comes to overcoming addictions, confronting our dark sides, and pursuing more positive life habits. Cultures that shy away from helping people address their behaviors fail them as environments of growth. Separating lip service from life inspection is spiritual suicide. Genuine spirituality lives and flourishes only in cultures and relationships of accountability.

Jesus adopted a very intentional approach of addressing behaviors in his teaching ministry. He would issue a command ("Love your neighbor") and then back it up with clear behavioral application (the story of the Good Samaritan). He made it clear time and again that his followers would be known not just by their attitudes and beliefs but also by their actions. Those of us who claim to be his people dare not miss this central truth. This is why one church seriously pursuing a people development culture is training a cadre of spiritual coaches equipped to help people identify their life growth agendas, specifically focusing on behavior. They help people identify behaviors that accelerate their growth as well as those that sabotage their life progress.

## From Curriculum-Centered to Life-Centered

In the program-driven church, people development efforts tend to focus on curriculum. In this curriculum-based approach, we study the Bible rather than allowing the Bible to inform us. We produce countless sermon series and Bible class materials and small group studies, all abetted by a Christian publishing world that requires sales for survival. The result is that we process people through curriculum that is often seemingly unrelated to real-life situations. Then we ask them to make the often difficult connection, taking what they have "learned" and applying it to their lives. This is backward. If you help people examine their lives, figure out what's going on, and distill out the issues, you've prepared the seedbed where learning and application can occur.

Cathy, my wife, has been helping a family deal with unusual and trying circumstances. The mother gave birth to five boys at the same time (especially unusual considering that no fertility medications were involved). She was already the mother of two boys, one of them just a year old, so the impact of this event has turned her life upside down. Cathy has been helping organize support for this family, everything from baby supplies to an extreme home make-over to equip their home to handle the quints. She received a call one morning from a well-meaning lady who announced that she wanted to take the mother out of the house one hour a week to "mentor her" with a Bible study. Cathy responded, "Why don't you just come over and fold diapers for one hour a week? When Mary and I are folding diapers and feeding babies, we talk about everything." That's life-centered development.

## From Growing into Service to Growing Through Service

Another notion tightly bound to the idea of how people develop is at odds with program-driven church practice. In the program church, the assumed path toward maturity essentially involves starting by dealing with personal issues (family, spiritual, financial, emotional) and then progressing to helping others. This is why service to others is considered "graduate school" in this culture, a sign of those who are truly "committed."

The missional church assumes that service to others is the first step, not some later expression of spirituality. We all know that we grow the most when we are helping and serving others. Service is the threshold where many of us learn the most about ourselves and come to see God at work in the world. This is why people development cultures are aided by an external focus in ministry. This is a crucial link between the first two missional shifts.

Recently, I visited a missional congregation that is experiencing this linkage. Because of their emphasis on serving others, the congregants are witnessing remarkable stories of growth among their members, and not just adults. One dad told me about his third-grade daughter's decision to set up a lemonade stand to raise money for a family whose home had burned down. I met a high school sophomore who has launched a personal ministry of distributing prayer boxes in various places in his community, collecting and praying for these requests, and e-mailing follow-up notes of encouragement.

This bias toward growing through serving is why missional congregations and ministries deploy people into service as much and as soon as possible. Waiting on people to be "ready to serve" usually means preventing them from serving, since most of us learn by doing and debriefing rather than through training divorced from deployment. Jesus deployed his disciples long before they were "ready." He knew that the fastest way to develop them was to engage them in real ministry encounters. He then debriefed their experiences so that they could learn from those experiences.

## From Compartmentalization to Integration

In our discussion of the first missional shift, I noted that the externally focused church sees itself as deployed across all domains of culture already. Followers of Jesus work in health care, arts and entertainment, law enforcement, business, education—in short, in all sectors of society. God has positioned them there as missionaries to bless the world through them. This understanding recognizes an integrated approach on God's part to engage the world.

This perspective contrasts sharply with the typical internally focused church, which looks at the church's identification as one silo of culture, mainly preoccupied with church business.

The second missional shift provides a similar corrective to the ways the church has gone about developing people. The result of the program-driven church culture has been to aid the development of life compartmentalization. This is evidenced by people's segmenting their concepts of spirituality, including the famous sacred-versus-secular duality. In this perspective, church people have been able to do their church thing (where they consider spiritual things and engage in spiritual activities) while omitting any missional emphasis from much of the rest of their lives. So they wind up with a fragmented life of work, home, school, leisure, hobbies, whatever.

I recently saw a classic example of the compartmentalized bias of the church-centric church culture on television as I was watching a well-known and very fine pastor deliver a message in his church worship service. In a sermon dealing with spiritual gifts, he made the statement that unless people had identified a gift and were using it "at church," they weren't growing. Missional followers of Jesus understand that the New Testament discussion about gifts and ministry occurred in a world where acts of ministry were primarily done in the marketplace, not "at church." They were *being* church in the world. Those early followers of Jesus did not suffer from the nonintegrated dilemma facing contemporary church culture.

A people development missional agenda that is life-centered and service-oriented and practices ongoing life debriefing promotes an integrated life. In this approach, spirituality shows up at home and in the marketplace as well as anywhere missional followers of Jesus find themselves. This includes all life relationships, which are treated as kingdom opportunities. All life activity is considered kingdom investment. This perspective opens up the way to practice and to celebrate missional living, not programmed activity, as the true work of a missional community.

Two men named Mark, one a high-powered business consultant, the other a senior partner in a major law firm, embody this missional perspective as they pursue their lives as friends and followers of Jesus. They are part of a missional community that meets each week. During the week, Mark and Mark exchange e-mails with each other to share prayer requests, struggles, and achievements. They have positively implicated themselves into the lives of each other's kids. They are involved with various community charities. They work together on projects executed by the missional community they are a part of. They are accountable to each other for how they treat their wives, their employees, their customers, and their friends. For them, like other missional followers of Jesus, *church* is a verb—a verb of being—that integrates life.

## From Age Segregation to Age Integration

The program-driven church has created separate generational silos in the church experience, from worship services to religious education to activities, even community service and mission engagements. It is quite possible for families in the program church not to share any common experiences during a day at church. This may keep consumers busy, but it doesn't do a thing for people's development. People often grow more in intergenerational environments. That's why God created families. We come into this world and learn our most fundamental life lesson in an intergenerational setting. There is something profoundly abnormal going on when spirituality is detached from this natural dynamic.

For years, I have encouraged student groups to quit taking "youth" missions trips and instead promote family experiences in these settings. I have done this not only to promote intergenerational connections but also because many young people need and desire some contact with older people who have both skills and wisdom. On the flip side, many senior adults are helped in their own sense of legacy when they discover the interest that younger generations have in them. When Hurricanes Katrina and Rita created the need for massive disaster relief efforts in New Orleans and the Gulf states, many response teams were intergenerational. The surprising discovery for many was that when these groups came home, teenagers and seniors had often developed great relationships and had become "best buddies."

One of the key ways that children's and student ministers can help families is to help them conduct God conversations at home, across the generations who live there. (Unfortunately, the program church has promoted church conversations—"How was your Sunday school? Your youth service? Are you going Friday night?"—but not God conversations.) One student leader e-mailed the parents of his students every week. In the e-mail, he briefly summarized his teaching in the youth service, followed by several questions for the parents to use if they wanted to have some follow-up conversations with their teenager. Brilliant! Spiritual formation, outsourced to the church now for decades, must and can be reclaimed by families as something central to their life together.

Certainly all of us enjoy doing things with people who are our same age. But when it comes to developing fully as human beings, the range of human ages and issues across generations comes into play.

A friend of mine serves on various boards working for literacy among children and a better quality of life for teenagers. He happens to be in his seventies. In a recent conversation, he admitted that dealing with children on a policy level was no substitute for engaging personally with real live kids. He doesn't want to miss out on the greatest blessing—people!

## Some Further Thoughts

A couple of observations need to be made as I conclude this description of the missional shift from programs to people as the core activity of the community of faith. Each of these could warrant an entire chapter of its own. They are far more important than the treatment I can give them here.

First, a key to all we have discussed in this chapter is *relationships*. It is not possible to promote a people development culture without an intentional focus on relationships. It is the point, but it also helps you get to the point. Each concern I have identified, whether it is the need for life coaching or the creation of an environment that is life-centered or the need for intergenerational engagement, calls for relationships. People do not exist apart from relationships. They come to be who they are in relation to others. Only a church that ceased to be about people and became about an institution apart from people needs to be reminded of this. The missional church *is* people; it's not a place where people congregate.

Second, all of the discussions of this chapter have focused on how church environments can become more centered on people development. The reason for this focus is obvious. However, this shift, paired with the first move toward a more external ministry, means that people development becomes the core activity of our community engagement. The implications of this push us beyond drive-by blessings into serious and intentional efforts to develop the people we serve. If we help distribute food, we also convene educational opportunities for parents and try to create microeconomic development for people who need a leg up. If we tutor third-graders, we are also paying attention to ways we can bring ESL to their parents or offer life skill classes as part of our relationship with the school population. The bottom line is that this shift has to inform the application of the first one.

God is not confused about his intentions. He fights against everything that diminishes life. He has spared nothing, not even his own Son, to secure a better existence for humanity. The missional church ventures into the world as partners with God on his redemptive mission.

That redemptive mission has people squarely in its crosshairs.

# 6

# CHANGING THE SCORECARD FROM MEASURING PROGRAMS TO HELPING PEOPLE GROW

The second shift of the missional church—helping people grow—is the most challenging. The good news is that people are desperate for this kind of help, as we discussed in Chapter One. God has created a cultural milieu where people are clamoring to grow. The even better news is that life is what Jesus came to give—and an abundant life at that. That was his primary agenda. It still is. People are built to last!

Moving in this direction, however, calls for us to get out of the church business and into the people business. But for this to happen, we're going to need a new scorecard that celebrates investments in people, not just programs, and cheers break-throughs in people's lives, not just organizational achievement.

We need a scorecard that supports a people development culture.

## The Challenge

I recently met with a group of top-flight leaders of successful program churches who are committed to participating fully in the missional renaissance. We spent some time discussing the differences between a program-driven scorecard and a people development scorecard. As a group, they agreed with the sentiment that this shift will be the biggest challenge for new benchmarking in the missional church in North America.

Here are a few of the distinctions they uncovered, just to show how big a challenge this is. In the program-driven church model, the activities and numbers center on the following:

- Number of people involved, attending, or participating
- People recruited for church services
- Church activities
- Spiritual disciplines
- Money gathered and spent on church needs
- Church turf
- Church-centered "opportunities for growth"
- Staff devoted to program management

They contrasted this list with the scorecard that would be in place to celebrate a people development culture, including but not limited to the following:

- Relationships that people are intentionally cultivating
- People released into service
- Personal life development
- Money spent on people rather than buildings and administration
- Life turf (home, work, school, community, and so on)
- Life-centered growth
- Staff engaged in coaching people for their personal development

These are huge shifts. We know how to do the first list; we've been at it for decades, centuries in some cases. The second list demands radically different approaches that create a different agenda for the church and church leaders. It necessitates and is predicated on a moving away from the current program fixation. The people development approach reflects an understanding that the church in its essence and highest expression is incarnational, not institutional. The new measures therefore have to center around improving lives. The indicators cannot stop short of actually looking for a result that is expressed through a person. They have to move us past the belief that keeping people busy in church programming is the answer to their life development. This rescorecarding is not easy. If it were, we'd already be doing it! But we've got to keep trying—people's lives are at stake.

## Reallocating Resources

To pull off this new scorecard will require a retooling, a reallocation of every resource the church and church leaders employ. It can be helpful for us to think through the same grid of resources that we identified in thinking through the first missional shift: prayer, people (leaders and others), calendar (time), finances, facilities, and technology. In each of these areas, we can and should identify specific results in people's lives that would signal genuine progress for them (for instance, how many better marriages can we report this year?). We can also identify some corporate and organizational reallocation of resources that would help us realize a personal development culture (for instance, tracking the number of staff hours spent in personal coaching).

The ideas offered here are not designed to be the new scorecard. The goal is to stimulate your own imagination, maybe even to provide some menu options for you to consider as you move in this direction. The truth is, we're going to have to develop a track record in these pursuits in order to declare what they should be and what the best ones are. But we've got to get started. In fact, that's the best way to read this section—this is a starter set. You will do much better as you try these on for size.

## Prayer

I don't know a single leader who thinks we have enough prayer going on in the North American church. I know many who think, as I do, that this is one of the frontier areas of spiritual growth that has the most room for development. It is unfortunate that so many people think only of prayer as a spiritual discipline. It is this but so much more. It is breathing to a Jesus follower, the lifeblood of staying connected throughout the day to the heart of the missional God. If we pursue prayer as a discipline to be mastered, we tend to see it as something we do when we shut out the world and retreat into our prayer chambers. Missional Jesus followers certainly do engage in concentrated prayer like this, but they also pray with their eyes wide open as they move through their day. They don't want to miss what God is up to in the middle of life.

Perhaps we think because we pray in worship services and open and close our church meetings with prayer and offer classes in prayer that the people in our ministry constellations know how to pray. They don't. Just yesterday, I heard a church leader share a story that proves the point. A church member approached him on a Sunday after a worship service with the request, "I need a prayer." Thinking that the man meant that he needed the pastor to pray over him, the pastor asked him what he could pray for. The man replied, "No, I don't need prayer; I need *a* prayer." He then went on to say that he had been asked for a prayer by someone in need the previous week. However, he didn't know how to pray, so he told the person that he'd get a prayer and get back in touch! (The pastor took full advantage of the moment to do some fast prayer training.)

As a developmental resource for people, some things to measure might involve the following metrics. I am aware that these items do not address the quality of prayer per se; however, moving our praying more into synch with the heart of God is itself an improvement in the quality of our prayer.

- Number of people reporting that they are growing in their prayer life
- Amount of time spent in prayer during corporate church gatherings, including group and individual prayer as well as corporate prayer
- Amount of time spent in prayer as part of committee or work team meetings, with special emphasis on connecting the work of the group with the mission of God
- Time spent in prayer in staff meetings
- Number of specific people being prayed for both inside and outside the church
- Number of people prayed with during the week by church members
- Number of people serving as prayer partners for community leaders
- Number of church leaders with a prayer team interceding for them
- Number of prayer meetings conducted on church property
- Number of prayer meetings conducted in community settings
- Number of prayer answers reported
- Number of prayer cards received from community and business prayer boxes

## People

This category of resource reallocation might seem redundant at first blush, since people development is the point. However, the new scorecarding here needs to track how leaders and others are being deliberately engaged in people development processes. A look at some measurement possibilities can stir your own imagination to think about how rewarding certain activities can spur greater intentionality in the area of helping people grow.

## Ministry Constituency

Keep in mind that ministry constituency includes both people who are a part of our church group as well as the people to whom we are ministering in the community.

I find that it helps to think in terms of four categories when it comes to helping people grow in their individual lives. Any number of templates can be adopted here, but I offer the one I use when I coach people. I help them think through their lives in four areas: self-awareness, skill development, resource management, and personal growth. Self-awareness involves exploration of concerns such as family-of-origin issues, boundary setting, handling tough emotions, fostering emotional intelligence, relational health, strength awareness, personality identification, spiritual temperament, and key life events.

Skill development includes both life skills and job skills. Life skills deal with major roles we fill and life stage demands such as family roles as well as positions of leadership outside our families. Job skills can range from technical abilities to specific abilities we need to improve in order to perform our work better.

Resource management for people involves the realms of time, money, and mental and physical fitness. Self-management in these areas poses one of the most significant challenges for people in keeping them from experiencing the life they want to have. Many people sabotage their fulfillment with poor behaviors in one or more of these key aspects of life.

Personal growth development delves into lifelong learning (and unlearning), spiritual disciplines and formation, intentional debriefing rhythms, mentoring and being mentored, and family and relational health. These are huge categories to explore, but helping people become more intentional requires that we help them evaluate each of these issues and decide on some plan of improvement for each.

Engaging people in these areas might yield some of the following metrics, along with decisions about who is reporting to whom and how this feedback is captured. It could be that a template of predetermined "outcomes" would be developed for various environments and constituencies. You might have one or more scorecards for what you want to accomplish in people development with those you are ministering to in your external venues. There would be a different set of metrics tracking the personal development of people who are a part of the church already. The following benchmark suggestions are just that, ideas to prime the pump of your imagination as you determine to cultivate a people development culture.

- Number of people reporting improved marriages over time
- Number of people reporting improved friendships over time
- Number of people reporting increased friendships over time
- Number of people reporting improved family life over time
- Number of people engaged in financial planning
- Number of people receiving life coaching
- Number of people engaged in strengths identification and development
- Number of people who have created and are following a life development plan
- Number of people serving other people in some venue
- Number of people practicing intentional blessing strategy for those around them
- Number of people being mentored
- Number of people serving as mentors
- Number of people able to articulate life mission
- Number of people able to articulate core values
- Number of people reporting improved spiritual life over time
- Number of people growing in financial giving to kingdom causes
- Number of people debriefed in life experiences each week or month

- Number of people pursuing job skill development
- Number of people pursuing life skill development
- Number of debriefing exercises in corporate gatherings
- Number of debriefing exercises in small group venues
- Number of people reporting addiction recovery progress

### Leaders

Of course, all the possible metrics just listed can be tracked in the lives of those serving as leaders. In fact, one of the key needs of the North American church context is to figure out ways to keep from viewing leaders as mere "resources" that are used and instead figure out ways that they can grow through their service. Asking the kinds of questions we've just discussed as part of leadership development will ensure that leaders keep life in leadership!

Through their actions and engagements, leaders also play a huge role in creating and promoting a people development culture. Here are some possible ways to track the intentionality of this agenda.

- Number engaged in life coaching or mentoring
- Number of people being coached or mentored by each leader
- Number of staff and leadership meetings given to life and leadership debriefing
- Number of leaders who have developed and are pursuing an intentional learning agenda
- Number of programs operating with intentional developmental practices
- Number of coaches developed and deployed to deal with life issues such as marriage enrichment, relational health, and financial planning

## Calendar (Time)

Each of the metrics mentioned so far involves the use of time as a resource in developing people. Yet there are some specific scorekeeping benchmarks that deserve attention.

- Amount of time spent debriefing people engaged in community service
- Amount of time spent in leadership meetings given to the people development agenda
- Time reallocated to people development from reconfigured programs
- Progress on simplification of the church calendar by scheduling fewer events, meetings, and programs to free up time for people development efforts
- Time spent mentoring people in the community beyond the church
- Percentage of time in corporate gatherings spent celebrating faith stories
- Number of life story interviews included in sermons connecting ideas to people's experience and application
- Number of hours people report in community service directly related to people development (mentoring, tutoring, homeless ministry, and so on)

## Finances

We all know that people's use of their money reflects their core values. We also know that people make decisions in this area that lock them into living contrary to those values. Our financial decisions often become the tail that wags the dog, whether corporately (many building programs do this to churches) or individually. Here are a few benchmarks that can be tracked to see if people are growing in this important area of life. I've also included a few scorecard items for your church or ministry commitment to people development in the area of finances. Many of these can also be included in developmental goals for people you engage with your external ministries.

- Reducing corporate debt to free up dollars for people investment
- Amount of seed money invested in microeconomic development such as grants for inner-city projects
- Number of financial planning and management courses offered online and in personal coaching venues
- Number of people participating in financial planning and management offerings
- Number of people reporting personal debt retirement
- Amount of debt retirement by people in your ministry
- Number of people increasing their generosity through charitable giving
- Amount of giving recorded by constituents
- Number of families teaching their children financial lessons
- Number of teenagers involved in financial planning
- Number of messages (sermons, Web site, small group lessons) dealing with money issues (not just giving but dealing with financial matters across the board such as personal and family budgeting and estate planning)
- Number of people reporting they have drawn up a will
- Number of people reporting they have done estate planning
- Number of people reporting they have developed a personal or family budget

## Facilities

At first blush, you might wonder how buildings relate to creating and supporting a people development culture. The impact is felt in a number of ways, all the way from building designs that either discourage or encourage conversations to debt structure that leaves too few dollars for people ministry to the decision of where your ministry chooses to have physical space (a campus, multiple campuses, shopping centers, downtown community centers, and so on). One church I just heard about is combining its resources with the local YMCA to create a community center where the church has its offices in the Y and offers tutoring, after-school programs, and all kinds of volunteer engagement with people in a place where people are already gathering.

Some ways to measure a commitment to shift into more intentional people development rather than having the facilities merely play the role of supporting church programming might include the following:

- Percentage of facilities used during the week by people for personal growth (exercise classes, tutoring, skill seminars, and so on)
- Number of external or additional venues the church is creating for ministry, such as coffee shops or prayer booths
- Number of schools using church facilities for their activities
- Number of community organizations using facilities for their ministry to people
- Space devoted to conversation-friendly areas

## Technology

Technology used to support ministry. Now it creates and delivers ministry. The options and opportunities to help people grow through technology are staggering. Consider just a few metrics to chart your commitment to people development, both inside and outside the church. You will undoubtedly come up with many more.

- Number of personal growth opportunities (including spiritual curriculum) offered on your Web site
- Number of people engaged in online learning at your Web site

- Implementation of online coaching or mentoring
- Number of life change stories on your Web site
- Number of people engaged in spiritual discussions on your Web site or related blogs
- Number of people receiving training in personal use of technology
- Initiative to create online social space for ministry constituents (Facebook, MySpace, and so on)
- Creation of "need and lead" connections for people, allowing people to post needs (I need a job, a car, whatever) with the chance for people to respond (I know about a job, I have a car, I have money to invest in your business, for example); this can happen online but also on church bulletin boards
- Number of computers distributed to school-age children
- Number of computers recycled from businesses to people who can't afford them

Use the items listed in the six resource areas to prime your pump as you establish accountabilities and intentions to move more proactively into creating a people development culture. Remember, what gets rewarded gets done. Publish what you are tracking, just as you publish attendance and offering figures. That very act will not only inform people but also help them establish some growth areas for themselves.

## Getting Started: A Case Study in Conversation

To change a culture, you have to change the conversations. This is true in businesses, in politics, in a family, and in a spiritual context. This is why consultants help business leaders revision their work, why political advisers worry so much about spin, and why counselors spend so much time helping clients find new language to talk about their problems. This reality should cause spiritual leaders to think long and hard about the culture we are creating by what we say and how we say it.

You might consider conducting a communication audit to look at the content or your gatherings, Web site, and publications. Listen to your worship service announcements and your teaching messages. Are you communicating an externally focused ministry and a commitment to people development? Monitoring and shaping conversations is never more important than when we are leading a significant or directional change. Unless our conversation changes, people in our leadership constellation will not believe it. This is why the move to a people development culture requires a shift in conversation. Rather than always reporting in our gatherings on the state of "the church" or its programs (worship attendance, what's on the calendar that needs support), the content of announcements, testimonies, lessons, and sermons has to change.

One church I have worked with closely over the past few years is Peninsula Covenant Church in Redwood City, California. Gary Gaddini leads a wonderful ministry team there. This is a church community located south of San Francisco. It is a successful flagship program church in the region with a rich history and a great heart for making a difference in the community. It is engaged in a number of initiatives that has congregants involved in everything from city planning to schools to housing to recreation. As they worked through the implications of making the missional shift from a program-driven agenda to a people development agenda, the staff and leaders made a commitment to signal this directional change by holding personal conversations with members about the church—in this case, "the church" being the people who are the church.

The team did a great job. In a project called Real Talk, team members posted interview questions in bulletins, on their Web site, and in their class handouts. They created skits for their

Sunday worship services to publicize the conversations. They invited people to sign up as individuals or couples. They offered to go to lunch, visit homes in the evening, meet in coffee shops during the day, even talk during church time when people were already present. They wanted to make the opportunities as convenient as possible. They trained the interviewers on how to listen and when to speak.

In the guided conversations that the leaders (pastors and lay leaders) had with several hundred of their church members and participants, including teenagers, they used five questions. I will list each question and then indicate the rationale behind it so you can see the link to the people development strategy.

*What do you enjoy doing?* Besides being a good way to open a conversation (people love to talk about what they love!), this was designed to help people grasp an important truth. Many people have never made the connection that what they enjoy doing just might be the way God wants to bless people through them. A lot of church attenders think that spiritual service has to be hard or distasteful or else it doesn't count! These conversations helped many people see that God could use them in their everyday lives, doing the things they love doing, to expand the kingdom.

*Where do you see God at work right now?* One of the goals of spiritual formation is to help people see God at work in their lives. In our dichotomized sacred-secular approach to spirituality, we have trained people to look for God when they are at church or doing spiritual activity but not anywhere else. This question was designed to help people learn to look for God in their children, their neighborhood, the office cubicle next to theirs, wherever.

*What would you like to see God do in your life over the next six to twelve months? How can we help?* This conversation accomplished several things. It allowed people to talk about the things that were most on their mind, which is the entrée for most people to talk about their personal development. It also established a coaching environment and relationship that could be expanded (the church is working on this as a follow-up). And of great importance, the question signaled to people that *they*, not church program success, were the new scorecard. How they were doing and the progress they made became the new measures of the church.

Some people reading the second part of the question might wonder if it feeds the notion of church as a vendor of religious goods and services. The way the leaders handled the conversations avoided that impression. They used the responses to help people find the connections they need for growing, pointing them even to resources outside their church. This part of the conversation enabled interviewers to telegraph the willingness of spiritual leaders to help shape, not script, people's spiritual journeys. They did not rob people of their need to assume responsibility for their own development.

By the way, armed with this information, the staff are in a much better position to know what kinds of developmental opportunities they need to plan. The typical church program approach has calendar planning followed by frantic efforts to make sure people support the agenda. Responding to what people say they need in order to grow places the staff in a much different role and greatly lowers the "marketing" needed to get people to participate.

*How would you like to serve other people? How can we help?* This question pair capitalized on the truth that most people grow the most through service. The ensuing conversation also helped link people to the external shift, because the gist of the talk was about helping people outside the church, not about finding a way to "plug them in" to church service opportunities (though some of that occurred). The responses also helped church leadership figure out how the Spirit was calling the church out into the community (if you have forty people wanting to tutor kids after school, this tells you something about the pathway into the community you want to pursue). The discussion generated by this question also helped some people figure out how they could bless people through what they enjoyed doing. Another benefit was helping the staff know what kind of training people needed in order to become better servers.

*How can we pray for you?* The conversations ended with prayer informed by the person interviewed. Some people broke down at the end, saying that they had never felt as cared for as they did in this experience. In some cases, prayer needs were also passed along to the pastors on staff and to the prayer ministry team of the congregation (always with permission) so that others could join in the effort.

I asked John Seybert, the executive pastor at Peninsula Covenant Church, to summarize the impact of Real Talk. Here's what he said:

> Our Real Talk experience provided us [with] a short-term benefit and a long-term benefit. In the short term, we connected with people and took the spiritual pulse of their lives in a way that no program (survey, questionnaire, etc.) could have done. The conversations allowed us to see that people had passions, interests, and existing involvements but that they weren't necessarily connecting them with God's presence in their lives. Although the data wasn't meant to be used to draw concrete conclusions and launch more activities, we recognized themes through the conversations (busyness, importance of children and family, etc.). In hindsight, it's no wonder our Beautiful Days [catalytic community blessing events focused on elementary schools] are so well received, because they hit a nerve with people and their desire to serve others, especially children.
>
> The long-term outcome of Real Talk is the emphasis we have begun to place on coaching. We are beginning to focus our people development resources on implementing coaching networks built around life's common issues (finances, marriage, children, etc.) The ability to mass-customize people's development and the increased "stick-to-itiveness" of development through coaching are key reasons we are shifting in this direction.

The scorecard that this particular church is developing relies heavily on the wealth of insight gained by actually having intentional conversations with its people.

Helping people get a life is the hardest work God does. That's true for us as well. Partnering with him on this mission signs you up for disappointment, challenge, pain, grief, and loss as you deal with people. But it also sets you up for exhilaration, joy, hope, and abundant life. That's life. And that's the point.

# 7

# MISSIONAL SHIFT 3: FROM CHURCH-BASED TO KINGDOM-BASED LEADERSHIP

The e-mail came just ninety minutes before I headed overseas. "There are a lot of people upset at what you are doing," it began. At the time, I was leading a visioning project for my denomination. The e-mail sender was writing to express his (and purportedly many others') disapproval of my efforts.

My first thought was, "God, why couldn't you have held this e-mail off for another two hours?" By then I would have been gone and not seen this feedback for another ten days (this was in the ancient days before the proliferation of Internet cafés, cell phones, and text messaging). As it was, I couldn't do anything about it except carry its burden into vacation. I sent a reply that acknowledged the e-mail and our need to talk after I was back in the country.

The problem was, even though the e-mail was sent, it was not gone. Not from my mind. Throughout the flight, I obsessed over the correspondence. I mentally composed dozens of replies defending my work, countering my detractors' objections. Three days into the trip, still brooding over the e-mail, I admitted to my wife, "I can't get over that e-mail." Her response startled me. "What if he is right?" she asked. She saw my puzzlement, so she pressed further. "What if a lot of people really are upset? Would you do anything differently than what you've done?" "No,"

I replied. "Then what's the worst thing that could happen—you lose your job?" she responded. "Do you think God would take care of us?"

In a matter of seconds, Cathy's probing clarified the real issue feeding my irritation and defensiveness: fear! I was afraid. The e-mail had threatened my security by alluding to the dissatisfaction of "a lot of people." Once Cathy pulled the dragon out into the light of day, I could see that it was toothless. I was able immediately to put the issue to bed. Fear when confronted often loses its grip.

The enemy of our soul loves to whisper fear into our spirits. He amplifies the sound ("there are a *lot* of people upset") to create as much terror as possible. But once you pull the curtain back, you discover a much diminished threat. The Lord knows our plight in this regard, which is why "fear not" is the most often repeated command in Scripture.

I know that the themes I address in many of my seminars raise the anxiety level of some people in the audience. I have found that for some, the background noise of fear is so loud in their spirit that they become unable to hear the Spirit. Often I swill ask people to share their fears with a colleague next to them and receive a prayer of encouragement. The relief in the room is sometimes palpable, and participants become more relaxed as they consider the future. The fears that are shared in those encounters reflect a similar set of issues.

I don't know my role in this new world.

I don't know how to make a living if all this all true.

I don't know if I have the competencies I need to function in a missional environment.

I don't think I can lead this transition.

I don't know what to do to get started.

[You might understand their fear. Maybe you are experiencing it too. Perhaps your anxiety or even anger (often the way fear manifests) has gotten to the point that it will be difficult for you to hear what I am saying in this chapter. The questions in the back of your brain are just screaming too loudly for you to hear anything else. Let me suggest that you flip to the back of this chapter to the section titled "Frequently Asked Questions." You might find something there to quiet your spirit. You can then resume your reading right here where you left off.]

These fears are leadership issues. And they are real. They anticipate the third shift necessary for you to join the missional renaissance. It is the move from church-based leadership to a kingdom-based leadership. The latter is the kind of leadership that fosters the first two missional shifts. This shift is the leadership response to the challenges of developing an externally focused ministry and shaping a people development culture.

## A.D. 30 Leadership

Church-based leadership is well entrenched, courtesy of the Constantinian world order, resulting in a clergy-dominated church culture. This kind of leadership can be described as institutional, maintenance-oriented, positional, pastoral, church-focused, and highly controlling. Kingdom-oriented leadership is more akin to the kind of leadership we see at work in the early days of the Christian movement, in its apostolic era. A different set of descriptors captures the character of this leadership: organic, disruptive, personal, prophetic, kingdom-focused, empowering.

What I used to call "apostolic leadership" was problematic for some people. Some confuse it with the gift of apostleship that is variously treated by different religious traditions. So I changed the label to "apostolic-era leadership" to try to communicate a character and content of leadership that reflects what we see operating in the New Testament. That change in designation still didn't do it for some people who wanted to translate the earmarks of this leadership into existing church roles. In other words, some saw the description as merely calling for different behavior on the part of church-based leaders. What I am looking for is a way to talk about leadership that transcends traditional clergy roles but doesn't deny their importance, that can incorporate new expressions while retaining current practices, and recaptures the essence of the unchanging mission as it morphs forward into the emerging culture. In short, we're talking about leadership that is both worthy of the Christian movement and competent to pursue its agenda.

Increasingly, I am calling this "A.D. 30 leadership" to acknowledge its origins and characteristics.[1] I didn't pick this era because it was an idyllic time. Hardly. If the early church was as ideal as some people make it out to be, the New Testament would be a whole lot shorter! But it was an era with challenges very similar to those we face in our day. Both the first century and our own have spiritual landscapes distinguished by the death of the old gods, the collapse of institutional religion, the rise of religious pluralism, and heightened spirituality. And in both the apostolic era and ours, the Spirit has responded by raising up similar leadership. This is leadership that is typified by being mission-centered, kingdom-focused, entrepreneurial, profoundly spiritual, reproducing, and culturally connected.

When people consider A.D. 30 leadership, they tend to think only of Pauline apostolicity—the church planter and missionary to other cultures. But there was also the Petrine apostolic leadership. Peter's ministry focused on those already in the household of faith, brokering the new reality of the Spirit's work into the Jewish-Hebraic culture more historically connected to God's mission. Missional leaders can still be Pauline or Petrine. Some find that they can be missional only in new settings and are quite at home engaging cultures that are not culturally Christian. Other leaders are most comfortable and effective at home serving as missionaries to the church culture, challenging those in it to connect with the Spirit's agenda in the world beyond them.

But the bandwidth of A.D. 30 leadership is much broader than the original eleven apostles plus Paul. Lydia the merchant,

Steven the deacon, Onesimus the slave, Barnabas the venture capitalist, an unnamed Ethiopian government official, Timothy the pastor, Luke the physician—these are just a few of the leaders we meet from multiple domains of first-century culture who played significant roles in a typical apostolic function of opening up new territory for the gospel, both inside and outside the church.

Now as it was then, A.D. 30 leadership is not restricted to clergy roles, nor is it isolated in church. It is leadership that is deployed by God across and in every sector of society. A.D. 30 leaders perform their roles as viral agents in the place of influence already assigned to them in their life pursuits. It would be a huge mistake to assume that the following shift descriptions apply only to clergy roles. They detail a work of the Spirit that reaches across all walks of life, giving leadership to the movement.

## Shifting Leadership Gears

"I need to come see you," the pastor said over the phone. "If we are ever going to make the shift into being a missional church, I've got to figure out what I need to be doing." He had correctly assessed the leadership challenge; now he wanted some pointers for addressing the problem. Along with thousands of others who want to pursue a missional journey, he will need to move from primarily leading an institution to giving leadership to a movement.

The following shifts highlight key changes that must occur for kingdom-based leadership to emerge. Most of these shifts have to do with the leader's self-perception. Unless this changes, nothing else will. Some of these shifts address the scope and methodologies for training missional leaders. The discussion will frustrate those who want a plug-and-play model of leadership or leadership development. With each shift, you will have to figure out the implications, if any, for the leadership you are giving and the leaders you are trying to develop.

## From Church Job to Kingdom Assignment

In A.D. 30, no one had a church job. Leadership responsibility in the church did not play out then the way it has since. There was not a sense that church leaders served church members in a customer service relationship. They weren't consumed with building and operating the church as an institution. It was an organic movement multiplying in the streets. Leaders did what they did, whether preaching or pastoral care or whatever, for the sake of the kingdom movement. They wanted to make sure people knew about Jesus and understood the implications for being his follower. God was doing something new on earth, and the church was part of it.

God gave leaders as gifts to the church for its mission. Some leaders gave voice to the movement in public forums, articulating the truth of the gospel, sharing the good news. Others taught new followers the spiritual and lifestyle tenets of what it means to be a Jesus follower. Still others organized charity efforts within the community of faith, while some galvanized relief efforts for people in the larger community. Pioneer leaders extended the territory where the good news was shared. The kingdom of God was breaking through in unprecedented ways.

Then something happened. Actually, several somethings happened over the course of centuries. Church leaders became captured by the institutionalization of the church. Hierarchies of leaders developed with their efforts primarily focused on the church. This rise of a clergy class eventually turned the mission inward as the agenda of the kingdom of God yielded to ecclesiastical concerns. The biblical idea that followers of Jesus are called to live out his mission in the world became replaced by the substitute agenda of church members expressing their religious devotion through church activities superintended by clergy.

The missional renaissance calls out for a refocusing of church leadership to reflect once again God's vision for the mission of his people. Missional leaders cannot tolerate continued disobedience and apathy toward a kingdom agenda, an agenda that includes the church but extends to the world. These leaders may hold church roles, but they are putting new content into these roles. Missional congregational pastors now pastor the community, not just the church. They deliberately develop relationships outside their traditional church role, like Mac, who serves as chaplain to the employees of the largest employer in his town. Missional student ministers, like Jarrod, who pastors the high school football team, serve as church-sponsored missionaries to reach the teenagers in our culture. Missional children's ministry leaders, like Jamie, who organizes community service projects that families can do together, use their ministry venue to help families understand how to live missionally.

Some missional leaders forgo traditional church roles. Some take jobs to connect missionally with a culture that will never come to church. For example, Drew, a former church staff member, is now a department manager in a high-end grocery store in a city he feels called to serve. He has forged relationships with coworkers that have led to the chance to introduce them to Jesus. Their lives, like so many millions in our culture, are completely unattenuated to the frequency of church programming and scheduling. If they were ever going to meet Jesus, it was going to have to happen in the grocery store or at the bar after work. That's where Drew came in. And so did Jesus. Jacqueline, a former student minister, made a similar move to become a high school teacher so she could be intimately connected with the teen culture every day right where teens live.

Missional leaders are also emerging among leaders whose background never was clergy-related. They are business owners and community leaders who have determined to be missionaries in their primary sphere of influence. They don't want church roles or too many church program responsibilities. They are too busy ministering to the people who work with them every day. Marie hosts what she calls a weekly "lifetime" meeting with the hospitality staff of the restaurant she owns. She takes prayer requests along with offering some life skill training such as how to construct a personal budget. Tom has a Bible study time with his construction crews at lunch on Fridays. This puts him in immediate touch with the needs of his workers, many of whom are navigating the immigration and naturalization process. He offers ESL classes and coordinates training on how to get a driver's license. These are leaders in a movement. Their actions may not swell church attendance (in fact, church people would be highly upset if Marie's workers showed up on Sunday and left the restaurant dark!). But they usher in the kingdom in the world, right where people can get it.

## From Institutional Representative to Viral Agent

I have been privileged to work with the Army Chief of Chaplains Office at the Pentagon. During one visit just prior to the beginning of the Iraq war, our discussion focused on the spiritual competencies and challenges of the chaplaincy corps. Historically, the role of the chaplain has been to serve as a representative of the faith that people took with them into military service. However, the spiritual landscape among service personnel has changed significantly, particularly among younger recruits. Many of these soldiers are coming into service with no spiritual formation or religious affiliation.

This cultural shift makes the chaplain's role more apostolic. The situation calls for the gospel to be introduced to soldiers who don't know it. For many chaplains, this requires retooling their skills to respond to this new reality. They need new apologetic skills, including help in knowing how to direct conversations to a spiritual level. As one of the officers commented after a tour in Iraq, "The old adage that 'there are no atheists in foxholes' isn't true anymore. These soldiers aren't asking the same questions about life and death and what's next. They are nonchalant about eternity." Rather than waiting to be sought out by soldiers with spiritual questions, chaplains have to introduce spiritual topics proactively. Although their training is in teaching, their challenge is increasingly to live such exemplary lives that they woo soldiers to God.

It occurred to me only later that this same challenge applies to church leaders in North America. Most have been equipped to serve as institutional representatives for faith that people already possess. The challenge is to connect with a culture that is unacquainted with the good news of Jesus.

The default position for church leaders in North America is that of institutional representative. This is certainly how people outside the church perceive clergy, eyeing them with suspicion and an appreciation only slightly greater than what they feel for politicians. This disdain reflects their overall disconnect from the institutional church. These environmental conditions make it increasingly difficult to be a missionary while keeping a church job. Once people find out you work at a church, you suddenly have a lot of explaining to do and disclaimers to offer to gain further hearing. When I was a pastor, I found myself engaged in numerous conversations with people who shut down once they realized what I did for a living.

The understanding of church leader as institutional representative is even more pronounced inside the church culture. Church staff, and even many volunteer leaders, find themselves locked into project management and program development to produce the events listed on the church calendar. They recruit and train leaders for church work. They market the church internally to its members. "Don't miss this!" "Have you signed up for this?" "The church *this*" and "the church *that*" punctuates almost every conversation with members in this church-as-vendor-of-religious-goods-and-services culture. This situation is so prevalent that it feels normal. And that's the problem! Instead of being spiritual leaders in the kingdom of God, partnering with his mission in the world, we have created leaders to run the church.

Leaders of a kingdom movement see themselves in a far different light. They talk about God, not just about church.

And when they talk about God, they don't use the discussion as a way to get around to marketing their church. They view themselves more as viral agents (in a good sense). Just as viruses look for any way to gain entrance and infect a host, these kingdom leaders look for any way they can to gain entrance to people's lives to "infect" them with God's love for them. They may try airborne techniques (preaching, teaching), but they are not limited to these. They will look for human contact (caring, coaching) and even brokenness (mercy, compassion) as opportunities to demonstrate the kingdom. They are not stymied by opposition; they respond to challenges by looking for new ways to become even more potent kingdom agents.

Viral agents search for opportunities in the routines of people's lives. Day-care centers, schools, community baseball diamonds and parks, local health clubs, professional organizations, workplaces, art and entertainment venues—all are places where chances to be a viral agent abound. Viral kingdom agents also know that human need creates viral susceptibility—we are designed to "catch" the viruses. This awareness is why they tutor kids in schools, serve as volunteers in hospitals, work in food banks, and staff crisis pregnancy centers. They've taken leadership to the streets, literally. Congregations that are missional learn to celebrate this leadership choice by preparing people for their kingdom assignment and not tying them up with unnecessary club activities.

Smart missional leaders with church roles look for ways to be viral agents within the church community. They understand that the kingdom is both taught *and* caught. They search for ways to expose people in church to missional engagement. They make sure to celebrate those efforts so that others in the congregation get exposed. They will even use existing church programming to create a new viral outbreak.

As she contemplated how to help her church become more missionally engaged with the community, Chelsea came up with the idea of offering her church's services in providing a vacation

Bible school (VBS) for a day-care center located down the street from her church. Rather than trying to recruit kids out of day care into a church activity, she decided to take the church to them. The day-care facility enthusiastically embraced the idea. Though not all the kids participated (parents were informed so they could opt out if they wished), the overwhelming majority did. The positive experience and relationships established created even more possibilities of missional engagement between the church and the day-care center. As a starter, every day-care worker now has a prayer partner in the church.

Chelsea's move was also a brilliant way to spread the virus internally in the church. Vacation Bible school is a venerated program in her church (as in most churches). By attaching a missional emphasis to it, she greatly legitimized the church's journey into the missional renaissance. Because VBS generally attracts a number of older workers, many of the church's senior leaders were exposed to a positive missional experience. In addition, Chelsea took advantage of the opportunity to create some cross-generational engagement by pairing teenage workers with older adults. She boosted teen involvement by using VBS as a training opportunity for teenagers who were headed off on summer missions trips to conduct VBS overseas. This viral agent had strategically exposed her whole congregation to the missional movement. No vote or debate on the subject was required. But the positive experience has opened the door to a new world.

## From Director to Producer

This is an image I use a lot in my consulting to help church leaders understand their function as leaders of a movement. Hollywood directors are project managers. They work with all phases and components of filmmaking to produce a movie. They are on the set during every scene. They are in the film lab during editing. They are everywhere. Very little happens without the director's attention. Producers play a different role. They find great stories, recruit talent, raise capital, negotiate with studios, and hire directors to bring ideas to life.

Classic clergy church leadership operates in a director's mode. Not much happens without the ordained ones present. From ministering the sacraments and teaching to conducting worship and administrating the church, clergy can be found right in the middle. This is not bad. It just limits the ministry reach of the church. Come to think of it, that *is* bad!

Apostolic leaders in the New Testament found ways to release people for ministry. Whether it was the original crew faced with a food distribution crisis or a missionary from Tarsus managing a new church network, apostolic leaders understood the essential connection between the success of the mission and their willingness to launch other people into significant leadership roles. A failure to do this would have doomed the movement to be swamped by its early success. The apostles acted as producers.

Today's apostolic producer types can easily be spotted against the landscape of typical directors. Ministry doesn't collapse around them; it radiates out from them. These leaders create a culture of ministry and leader incubation that multiplies everyone's efforts. In short, they feed the movement. As one lead pastor of a large southern church told me, "I just love finding out every week some new ministry that our people are doing." That's a producer mentality. This pastor doesn't need to be the star of every show; he doesn't even need to show up at most episodes. He plays the essential part of empowering leaders to pursue their callings and passions. He strengthens others' obedience by creating a culture where they can say yes to the Spirit. And he celebrates the heck out of their successes. By the way, all the ministries he told me about happened away from the church. This same pastor went on to say, "I wouldn't have a clue how to do what they do." The very thought that clergy could preside over these kingdom expressions is ludicrous. Yet many congregational leaders do not trust people to minister out of their sight.

Directors coach people into church roles to star in the movies the church leaders are making. Producers release missionaries into the movement by helping them create and star in their own movies.

## From Reliving the Past (the Historian) to Rearranging the Future (the Journalist)

Typical church leadership spends a lot of time keeping the past alive. This shows up in everything from hanging on to outdated structures to preaching sermons and teaching Bible studies that leave God operating in ancient texts and stories. This is largely the result of a worldview of clergy that still have the church at the center of the universe. They mistakenly think that this church-centric approach is relevant to people's lives.

I just returned from a trip to Europe, the land of cathedrals. Excuse me, I mean the land of church museums. We were in a Swiss city on a church holiday. The faithful—all seven of them—were huddled together down front while the rest of us tourists wandered around reading historical placards detailing the life of the cathedral when it was the center of things. The clergy of the cathedral are still very caught up in its activity—and very separate from the real world outside the cathedral's grounds.

While we in the United States love to point to Europe to make us feel better about our participation rates, we need to heed the lesson. A faith built on dead people doesn't thrive. And when we come together for our gatherings, if all our heroes are the ones who've gone before and all our God stories are about yesteryear, we're in trouble.

Please don't hear what I'm *not* saying. Leaders of the missional movement still teach and preach the Bible. They appreciate the past. But they mine the past for lessons on how to forge ahead. Whereas the classic church celebrates textual exegetes, the missional movement yearns for journalists who can tell us what God is up to today.

This was the role of apostles and prophets in the New Testament. They witnessed and passed along God news that was good news. These journalists tied their stories to the work of God before, but they allowed the new developments to shape their understanding of God's work in the world. Examples of this abound. Just think about Peter's reporting of the Samaritan and Gentile Pentecosts. Both visits of the Spirit were unexpected and caused quite a stir. It was Peter's descriptions that helped the church make sense of what was happening. Or think of Paul's letters detailing the work of God among the Gentiles, shaping the early movement's character.

Recently, I spoke to a denominational gathering of pastors who come from a rich historical and theological tradition. I could see the participants selecting themselves into two groups. There were those who struggled to take everything I said and fit it into their existing doctrinal and methodological paradigms. By the time they finish doing this, the ideas I shared will be unrecognizable or dead. Sad, but these leaders prefer irrelevance and a ministry of hospice care to dying congregations. Fortunately, there was a far larger group of clergy in that audience who were hungry to know what God is up to and how they can get in on it. They wanted to report on it to their congregations so they could become engaged with it. They want to transcend their current roles. They are evidence that the Spirit has not given up on the North American church.

Journalists take us to places they've already visited. They uncover stories beneath the stories and inform us of what's going on. They shape our perceptions by what they have seen, experienced, and uncovered. They move us from where we are into a new reality. After shaping the news for his viewers, the iconic news anchorman Walter Cronkite always signed off with "That's the way it is."

Today my oldest brother leaves on a trip to a destination he has already visited. This time he's taking his kids and grandkids. "I just want to see *them* see it and enjoy it," he told me over the phone. By the time my nieces and their families get back from the trip, they will have their own stories of exploration and discovery. My brother's joy will have translated into new experiences that shape the future of his family.

God doesn't need us to conduct his mission. We can't pull off resurrection or life transformation, after all. It just brings him incredible delight to see us enjoy what he already knows about. That is the privilege of being his offspring. He has cut us in on the deal! Our discovery of what he is up to becomes the faith story that is prologue to our future.

Missional leaders experience what God is doing and then tell others about it. In this way, they act as journalists to help us experience it, too. This means they spend time with God in prayer, asking him to show them what he is doing. This usually crafts a very different agenda for them than just doing what clamors for attention in their inbox. And it means they immerse themselves in life. They journey out of the citadel into the streets. Missional leaders, in touch with God and with the world, speak convincingly of what the people of God must do. You will not be around such leaders long without learning that their heart is being shaped by their encounters. You will find your own heartbeat matching theirs.

## From Train and Deploy to Deploy and Debrief

The typical practice for preparing church leaders for their ministry roles proves woefully inadequate for developing kingdom movement leaders. Standard approaches to leadership training for clergy not only ignores biblical patterns but also violates even the most basic understanding of how people (and leaders) develop. The current preparation methodology follows a classroom and pretested certification model. How absurd! There is no correlation between earning high marks on academic tests and being able to lead people. Again, don't hear what I'm not saying. I have studied some myself and think we need *more*, not less, theological emphasis. But it's all a matter of how and when it's delivered. And to whom. Of course, some seminary grads turn out to be leaders. But by and large, they were leaders when they entered. Seminary training enhanced their skills but didn't provide them. We can no longer rely on the low percentage of leaders who make it through and the pathetic results we are reaping. We must abandon the train-and-deploy model.

How did Jesus train leaders for the movement? He used the deploy-and-debrief method. This approach allowed him to take some pretty unpromising and in some cases mercurial candidates and turn them into movement leaders. He invited them to observe what he did, promising them on occasion that they would and could do what they saw him doing. After long hours of ministry, he routinely debriefed the day's events and teachings. He sent his disciples out on assignments *before* they were ready, knowing they would make mistakes. He would then debrief their experiences to help them learn from those experiences. "This kind of demon-casting will require extra efforts." "What do you think I was talking about in that story?" "What are people saying about me out there?" "What were you guys arguing about on the way here today?" These questions created teaching moments. Occasionally, he pulled his leaders aside for more extensive debriefing. "Come away with me" was not an invitation to a deeper devotional life but a leadership summons to discuss the successes and failure of an early mission trip.

Movement leaders can and must still be prepared this way. Let's start with the seminary clergy-training level. Eventually, the strangulating hold of accreditation will further relax to allow training regimens to be offered alongside deployment, employing delivery systems that permit people to stay put in their communities of relationship and leadership influence. Those wanting theological education to prepare for church leadership roles will no longer have to disrupt their families, move and live as transients for three to five years to secure their academic prize, and then have to try to reestablish life and relationships in some new place. Online technology is already creating nonresidential alternatives to the typical approach of residential studies. Seminaries will still offer a residential track for those who prefer it, but the main delivery will shift to nonresidential students who access online teaching at their own pace while integrating what they learn into their everyday life and ministry. This will greatly increase the scope of theological education.

Just this week, I taught a group of upper-level master's and doctoral students. In the class was a sixth-grade public school teacher from Chicago who was taking advantage of that seminary's modular curriculum, allowing him to come and go with his life rhythms for short-term on-campus instruction. The training entities, including seminaries, who take leadership development seriously will increasingly insist and provide for a learning methodology centered on routine and episodic debriefs of life and ministry. This gets at what Alan Hirsch characterizes as leadership development "along the way."[2]

The doctor of ministry approach of weeklong seminars followed by assignments is moving to the master of divinity level. As the process unfolds, learners will be given more and more opportunity to shape their own learning path. They will not pursue their learning as privatized consumers but rather will be tethered to the school through a life and ministry coach (who may live near them, trained by the institution for this role). The learners will also be engaged in peer mentoring as part of their developmental path, debriefing their learning and experiences with other similarly tasked learning leaders. This nonprivatized leadership training in a learning community will keep the experience from being just another information transfer process. Degrees and certifications won't be mechanically passed out to people who successfully complete classroom assignments but awarded to those who prove their ability to lead by demonstrating actual competency and the requisite health and emotional intelligence to serve as spiritual leaders. Credentialing will certify a proven leader, not just a wannabe.

At the congregational level, leader development efforts will focus on creating a leadership community designed to help people become more effective at exercising their leadership gifts in the marketplace and other community sectors. Small business owners need a peer experience with others who are seeking to be missional in their business culture with their employees and customers. Educators in school systems need a chance to debrief their kingdom leadership efforts with other schoolteachers. Just imagine a church setting where part of people's developmental path included a routine review of their missional efforts in life. Business leaders, students, health care workers, and stay-at-home moms would meet to strategize missional living and to encourage one another in it. Congregational leaders who want to deploy kingdom leaders will see to this development rather than focusing only on training people to do church work. This approach will actually make the church a partner in people's kingdom efforts rather than a competitor for their time, money, and energy.

## From Positional to Personal

In the old world, leadership could rely mostly on positional authority. Hierarchical models of organizational life promoted this. But today, leadership is increasingly personal. The person occupying the role is evaluated in terms of suitability for being followed. The changing interface at the workplace brought on by organizational flatlining, accompanied by the shift in expectations of younger workers, has contributed to the sharp rise in this expectation of personal leadership.

This dynamic is true even in the most hierarchical of cultures, the military. Some years ago, I spoke at a gathering of Air Force wing commanders. Over two dozen generals convened to discuss how they could make some changes in the culture of the Air Force. A rise in the number of suicides, coupled with scandals at the Air Force Academy, had precipitated this conversation. My focus was to help them see that young airmen and airwomen were looking for leaders they could believe in and follow, not just obey. They need close-up and personal leadership.

The same is true when it comes to spiritual leaders. "Imitate me" (1 Corinthians 4:16) was the apostle's call to leadership training. This was not hubris in Paul. It was the height of accountability! What Paul was saying is, "If you want to experience what I experience, do what I do." "If my life appeals to you, here is the ticket for your own ride: you have to do what I do." Positionally ensconced but personally removed leaders don't inspire movements.

So the question for you and me in the missional renaissance gets pretty personal. Are we living what we're talking about? Are our own lives missional? Is there a spiritual attractiveness to us? Do we have the stink of Jesus on us? Are we willing to be accountable and authentic with our journeys? Are we willing to die—not just physically but to church ambitions and celebrity status? Are we frequently caught saying yes to Jesus? If we do say yes to Jesus, we help others in our constellations of influence make the same choice.

## Frequently Asked Questions

Whenever I talk about the implications for leaders and leadership in making these missional shifts, I get a set of questions that are now predictable. Perhaps you might need to go back and reread this chapter after you work through these frequently asked questions. I make this suggestion because I have found that some people are so stuck on the questions in the front of their minds they can't hear what I'm saying. If that's you, that's OK. You can do what they can't in seminar settings—just flip back and start over.

## "What is the role of the traditional church in the missional movement?"

Some people hear my comments on the missional renaissance as suggesting that the traditional church is going to fold. I have never said that, nor do I believe it will or should happen. What I argue is that we need to change the conversation about the church from "*what* is it?" to "*who* is it?" As long as we keep the discussion tied to its "whatness," we will keep the leadership efforts focused on building better institutions and limit ministry to those individuals who choose or are able to participate in an attractional program. If we can shift the discussion to "who," we can be free to explore how the church shows up wherever followers of Jesus live, work, and play. Efforts can shift to community and incarnational expressions of Jesus in all sectors of the culture.

Specifically to those with the traditional church mind-set, I have argued that we must expand the bandwidth of what forms church should take, including many noninstitutional expressions. Lots of people obviously like the current format. But forms of missional communities are developing and will have their own appeal. Instead of excoriating these developments, why not champion them? Why not realize that many people in our culture will never be reached with the good news if we rely purely on the current church model for delivery? I have also suggested that traditional churches need to make some significant shifts in their content in order to participate in the missional movement.

Here are a few significant roles the traditional church can play in the missional renaissance.

• Churches can function as intake and deployment centers for missional followers of Jesus. Many current followers of Jesus are attending traditional churches. They, along with those coming into faith across the threshold of traditional church expression, need to understand the call to live missional lives. Their answer to it needs to be celebrated even if it plays out outside the church ministry.

• The traditional church can serve as an umbrella organization for missional communities (MCs). As I have said before, the sponsorship of MCs will not hurt the church's bottom line—but it won't help either. The motive for moving this direction cannot be to build up *this* church but to build up *the* church. These MCs will reach people who are never going to attend a traditional church. That's usually understandable. But the church must also understand that many, if not most, of the people brought into the kingdom through MCs won't "grow up" and start attending church. This is hard for church people to swallow and is a real test of conversion to missional.

• There are several benefits to the traditional churches that choose to cooperate with this development. The MCs will provide ways for their members to engage in the ministry needs that the MCs will uncover. This will help those choosing to stay with the institutional church gain an outlet for their gifts and talents in the community, making heroes of some who want to be missionaries but don't want to forsake the established social networks they enjoy at their church.

A missional community I have been involved with has been able to connect a local congregation with several ministry situations, including adopting a low-income apartment for ministry. Not only did the church allow people in my MC to funnel money through it for tax credit, but it also deployed several senior adult ministry teams into the situation. One crew helped with construction of a playground; another held a garage sale to raise money to outfit the community kitchen; still others did odd jobs for people who couldn't afford to pay for repairs. This made some new ministry heroes the church could celebrate. The partnership between our MC and the traditional church has been a win-win.

## "How will you maintain doctrinal and biblical orthodoxy if you're all off in your own communities doing your own thing?"

Some variation of this question has been asked every time in history when the church has considered new ways of being. The missional renaissance is not a call for everyone to develop a personal theology. The church has the apostolic function of exercising doctrinal oversight. The historical church has received the Word of God and will ultimately judge ideas and concepts as permissible, questionable, or heretical. New pressures have always forced the church to consider new theological issues and practices. The collapse of the Roman Empire weighed on Augustine in the fifth century, prompting his prolific theological writing. The Reformation in the fifteenth and sixteenth centuries certainly spawned its share of new theological insight. The Pentecostal movement of the twentieth century helped reintroduce and reshape the discussion of the Holy Spirit's role in the believer's life. The current missional movement is generating new thinking and writing in many theological categories, from missiology to soteriology, as a kingdom-centric perspective replaces the church-centric lens through which we have looked at biblical texts. In every era, in every society transformation, the church has figured out its orthodox message and practice. It will again. After all, the same Spirit still shepherds it.

## "What is the role of clergy in the missional movement?"

The clergy have dominated church leadership for centuries. Clergy will still be important in the missional era; it's just that they won't be able to maintain their current position of signing off on people's ministry or scripting their spiritual journeys. The clergy will be valued for the following functions:

• *Teaching.* People still value good teaching and need theological perspective brought to their lives. Good teachers will continue to gain widespread distribution. The delivery and placement of teaching will continue to morph along with the technology for delivery. While teaching has been the main event in most churches, that may give way to celebration of life transformation and God stories, with teaching available in more ubiquitous, asynchronous (anywhere, anytime) modalities (podcasts and the like).

• *Life coaching.* People are increasingly intrigued and drawn toward help for their lives, not just through counseling but also in more proactive ways. Clergy who have skills for helping people with their lives will be in demand.

• *Missional strategies.* Clergy are in a perfect position to serve as missional strategists, brokering ministry services between congregations and the community they are in. One retired pastor spends most of his time helping members of the fifty-five-and-over crowd give missional expression to their lives. He is helping them connect their passions and talents to kingdom advance, literally by having face-to-face strategy sessions where they map out specific initiatives that will help them become more missional. Missional strategists focus on deployment and debriefing of members, helping them become part of a missionary force.

Missional strategists will also build networks of churches and community agencies and organizations to tackle issues that are bigger than any one entity can address. Jon Talbert is one example. He heads Beautiful Day (http://www.ourbeautifulday.org), a regional movement of churches in San Jose, California, whose combined ministries now raise tens of thousands of dollars and release thousands of volunteer service hours per year in projects ranging from community beautification to extreme home makeovers.

• *Training for missional community leaders.* As the church becomes more organic and multisite in its expression, the need for leadership will change and increase. Clergy who can recruit and train effective missional community leaders will be in demand. I had a call just this week from a historically important church that has come to grips with the implications of the missional movement and is looking for a pastoral leader who wants to go in this direction. "As you know," the caller said, "this kind of leader is hard to find in our traditional resourcing pools." Again, this function may have regional and not just congregational jurisdiction. It will transcend denominational affinity as well. This is the case everywhere this kind of movement is emerging. Many of these leadership roles can and will be shared with nonclergy. While it often still proves advantageous to set people aside to devote their full attention to these pursuits, nothing says these jobs need to be filled by clergy. One church employed a retired executive in the community ministry role, leveraging his well-established business network. The historical qualitative clergy-laity designation will shift to a more functional distinction that doesn't elevate or assign to clergy a higher status than to nonclergy.

## "How do I earn a living doing what you're talking about?"

I always applaud the person who verbalizes this question in a group because everyone is thinking it! First of all, not everyone will have to find new jobs to go missional. Many current church leaders will be able to maintain their current employment while leading their congregations and ministries to join the missional renaissance. Many who want to earn a full-time living in ministry will increasingly need to think of themselves as portfolio managers. They will need to have multiple income streams, as opposed to the congregational support model. This is certainly not a new model. Missionaries and many workers in missions and ministry agencies have raised their support for years.

Other funding options will also be explored. Some people will earn income from secular sources. This model has been called "bivocational." Others, especially those involved in missional community engagement, may be able to garner grants for funding their work. Then there will be those who will have individuals champion their cause financially, investing in them and their ministry projects. The Renaissance of the fifteenth century occurred under this kind of patronage sponsorship.

What I encourage leaders to do to prepare for this involves several pieces of advice.

• *Clarify your life purpose.* You'd better know what you want to accomplish so you don't sabotage your life purposes by how you earn income. This personal clarity of mission ensures that you won't let working hours and conditions get in the way of having the time and energy to pursue your life dream. Just this week, an e-mail from a pastor revealed that he had quit his church job for the same reason. It got in the way of his being able to be available to people he wanted to do ministry with—the nonchurched. You might think that most leaders understand and can communicate their life purpose clearly. Think again. I make it a practice that when people write me wanting me to recommend someplace they might serve, I ask them to send me a three- or four-sentence statement of what they want to accomplish. For many, this is a clarifying assignment. For some, it takes weeks or even months to figure it out and to be able to succinctly say it.

• *Find your voice.* You want to be able to explain to other people (including potential donors and those you are recruiting to join your mission) what your mission is. Commonly called the "elevator speech," you need to be concise and concrete so that others can grasp it quickly and easily.

• *Be sure you're employable.* If you are thinking you might one day want to switch from full-time ministry income, start preparing now. Make sure you have skills that are transferable to other lines of work. Don't wait until you need these to acquire them. Go online. Attend night classes at your community college. One leader bought a small blueberry farm and within just a few years began to generate enough income from it to fund his ministry. I run into people all the time who would quit their church jobs "if I could make a living doing anything else." People who do what they do because they are financially trapped lose a lot of the joy of service. This leads to burnout and bitterness.

• *Pay attention to your emotional and physical stamina.* Many leaders don't have the energy they need to make a change because they are physically and psychologically worn down or worn out. Take care of yourself! It will create the margin you need for dynamic and effective spiritual leadership.

• *Bone up on organizational transitional skills.* This is especially true if you have a church job and plan to stay where you are in leadership and transition your ministry into a missional expression. It's not easy. It won't be accomplished overnight. You need to study everything you can about managing change and transition. Educate members of your leadership corps to the psychological dynamics of transition so they aren't caught off guard by resistance you typically encounter when making major organizational changes. They need to know what to expect so they can support the direction you want to go.

## "What about my call?"

This question is a frequent follow-up (even pushback) to my suggestion that one's missional ministry may not be completely funded from pew offerings in a local church setting. My response to this concern is this: "Does your call revolve around a mission or a job?" Strange, isn't it, that we seem to have confused the two? They don't have to be mutually exclusive, of course, but do we really want to minimize the call of God down to a guaranteed employment contract and a regular paycheck? Unfortunately, our church culture has created this confusion. We help people feel "the call" into clergy roles that have been influenced by culture and religious tradition. Pursuing these ecclesiastical roles may or may not reflect a call of being set aside by God for some special use. It might just be an appealing career.

The Bible presents the notion that God does indeed call individuals to serve his people and to accomplish certain assignments in the world for him. Persons who feel this kind of call should pursue it no matter how they cobble together an income to support it. Those who feel this call order their lives around it and make life decisions, including employment, based on it.

This third shift in engaging the missional renaissance is by far the most personally challenging for many in church leadership. Moving from church-based leadership to kingdom-based leadership turns out to be a test of obedience, not just grasping a new idea. Are we giving the kind of leadership that turns people toward the mission of God? Do we have the courage to pursue the call to missional leadership even if our incomes are jeopardized? Are we willing to risk our leadership to lead God's people toward him? Are we content with assessing our ministry on how well we meet the expectations of those we lead, or is our greatest allegiance still reserved for following Jesus? It is impossible to lead others into this journey without ourselves being captured by the heart of God for his redemptive mission in the world.

In the second film based on C. S. Lewis's *Chronicles of Narnia*, subtitled *Prince Caspian*, Peter and his younger siblings are transported back to Narnia to fight another battle against evil, this time to liberate the Narnians from the infringing Telmarines. When Aslan finally shows up, he offers a chance for new beginnings for those who want to be transported to our earth. At a climactic moment, King Peter realizes that his job is done. He hands his sword to Prince Caspian, a clear signal that Caspian is the new ruler. Peter departs Narnia, leaving Caspian in charge.

As I reflected on this scene, I realized how it captures much of the dynamic of the required leadership for the missional movement. Like Peter, we have been summoned to a conflict that predates us and involves many players, some not from this world. Our decision to engage the forces at work inspires those who are trapped in a binding evil. They dare to believe that things can be different. The outcome of battle is secure, but it does not mean that we escape injury and harm in prosecuting the fight. We have our role, our moment, but our part is transitory. From the time of our initial engagement, the plan always is to hand off the gains and struggles to others.

The fight is not about us. It is not our kingdom. We labor for a King whose intentions are sometimes hidden. Yet he is committed to the struggle and has joined the battle himself. Knowing this grants meaning to our strivings and perseverance to carry on. We push forward in the face of both mystery and certainty. Just hearing "well done" from the King is reward enough.

# 8

# CHANGING THE SCORECARD FROM CHURCH-BASED TO KINGDOM-BASED LEADERSHIP

Andrew has resigned from his tall-steeple church to follow a call to lead a network of missional communities. His denomination is providing him with support for a year as an experiment in a different kind of "church planting." He has three communities in the early stages of community building. Andrew is discovering that the challenges of leading a movement are quite different from those he faced as a local church pastor. In an e-mail he writes, "I have to manage my 'church expectations' and unlearn some things from 20+ years of professional 'attractional' ministry. . . . It's not a fast process to engage everyday, real-life, outside-the-church-circle people and their needs. . . . It's different than the managing of programs and keeping 'unhappy Christians' at bay, which was more the process in the past. In some ways it's more taxing to mentor than to manage."

Like others who are making this leadership shift, Andrew is running into the reality that he has to develop a new scorecard. What he does, what he thinks about, how he processes his life and ministry all are affected by a radically different ministry agenda. Whether you are retaining your church role while attempting to shift your ministry agenda, striking out into new territory like Andrew, or striving to lead the movement as a lay-person, your scorecard needs to match your leadership challenge.

It should call attention to the issues and reward the actions that will support kingdom-oriented leadership.

I have found it helpful to approach leadership issues by thinking in four different areas: paradigm issues (how the leader sees the world), microskill development (competencies the leader needs), resource management (what the leader has to work with), and personal growth (the leader as a person). My discussion of the leadership scorecard to support the move from church-based leadership to kingdom-oriented leadership will follow this template. This chapter touches on some issues that you might want to consider in each area.

The way to shift leadership results is to change what leaders are doing and thinking about. Leaders have to live the change they seek. This is not easy; it requires ruthless self-management. This is where the resource template we used in the scorecard discussions of the first two missional shifts will come back into helpful play. Your leader scorecard will require a similar reallocation of resources (time, money, and all the rest) on a personal level that we discussed when rethinking how the corporate scorecard could be more missional. Here's how that works. Once you commit to a specific result in any of the following four leadership areas, you have to figure out how to focus prayer, people (relationships), time, money, technology, and facilities (including your personal property) to achieve the results you want.

Does this sound hard? You're right—it is. And that is why many won't make the necessary shifts in becoming a kingdom-oriented leader. But those who participate in and shape the missional renaissance do shoulder this tough assessment. They do not think it too high a price to pay to experience the kingdom wave.

## Paradigm Issues

"Open your eyes," Jesus admonished the disciples in the John 4 story of the woman at the well in Sychar, "and look at the fields." The disciples had trooped in and out of the village without engaging the indigenous culture, carefully keeping to the safe cultural confines of their anti-Samaritan bias. They didn't *see* because they weren't looking.

Paradigms are about the way we see things. And the way we see affects our thinking and our behavior as leaders. In the case of the disciples in John 4, their field of vision was limited to their internal group. The result? They missed what God was up to! The same is true for you. Whatever you as a leader are looking at is what you are working on. And the way you are looking at it will determine your approach to engaging it.

This entire book has been about shifting paradigms from a church culture to a missional movement. These shifts require that the leader see things a certain way. If you see yourself as a church leader in a church role working with church people to get church things done, you will behave accordingly. If your paradigm of what it means to be a faithful Jesus follower primarily involves being a better church member, you will center your efforts on church stuff. None of this is wrong. It is one way of seeing the world. It is a church-centric view. It is not missional.

By contrast, missional leaders see the world and their role in it very differently. If this is your paradigm, you believe you are on mission in the world and are partnering with God in blessing the people in your sphere of influence. You may have a church job that positions you to be able to recruit others to this point of view. You might own a small business or teach sixth grade or have any number of platforms that afford you a chance to bless people in a way that intrigues them to move to a deeper relationship with God. You view life as a mission trip and order your own life around that view. For you, following Jesus does not involve adding a set of activities to your life. Following Jesus is life itself.

Each of the following suggestions captures part of our discussion involving the three missional shifts. In each instance, you would need to consider how you would apply your personal resources of prayer, relationships, time, money, technology, and personal property to achieve the results you want. For instance, you won't develop relationships outside the church by sitting in your church office. You might need to join a health club or coach a Little League team. The reallocation of your resources for each item will establish the "metrics" you can use to keep track of your progress. Here are some examples of possible measures that reflect an intentionality of developing a missional paradigm for life and ministry.

- Number of growing relationships with people who are not Jesus followers
- Number of relationships with people who are not church people
- Number of personal relationships with other community leaders
- Intentional study plan that includes periodicals, books, blogs, Web sites, and podcasts for cultural exegesis—helping you *see* your harvest field
- A plan to debrief these cultural lessons regularly with other key leaders
- Number of venues for intentional personal service in the community
- Number of hours in personal service in the community each month
- Number of life-coaching relationships
- Regular commitment to debriefing your personal life with a coach or personal growth group
- Number of stories of external, missional experiences used in your speaking and writing

Now that you've seen how metrics can be derived for even "soft" goals, the rest of this chapter will simply highlight some specific areas for investigation, leaving the metrics up to you, since your own particular leadership role and situation need to be considered. Establish some benchmarks that can help you track your progress. For instance, "securing a personal coach over the next three months," "lose two pounds each week for the next two months," and "schedule a meeting with a financial adviser within the next two weeks" are measurable goals.

## Microskill Development

As Andrew discovered in his journey toward missional leadership, the skills involved in being a project manager and in being a life-on-life developer are different. The following are some key skills for missional leadership that you might want to add to the training that prepared you for church leadership.

### Coaching

*Coaching* is the current umbrella term for connecting with people (including leaders) to further their development. Cultivating a people development culture will require that you come up to speed on what is required to coach people effectively. One of the ways to learn about coaching is to get some firsthand experience by securing a coach for your own development. You can also read books on coaching from both secular and religious practitioners. Coaching training is also increasingly available for spiritual leaders in denominations and some professional ministry groups.

### Storytelling

This is a crucial communication capability for connecting with today's culture. People under thirty actually make meaning through story, much as some of us older folk made meaning if we could diagram a sentence or create an outline. Whether in written or oral communication, the ability to tell a good story determines how far you penetrate into the minds and hearts of the people you are trying to persuade. I have argued for interviewing people during sermons, which is a form of storytelling, to drive home behavioral and attitudinal change. Getting stories about challenges in your community, among senior adults or student populations, for instance, will garner and release a lot of resources. Sharing stories of people's personal struggles and triumphs will encourage people development. Resources for study range from books and articles to storytellers' conventions and seminars.

## Conflict Management

The level of change introduced by the move to missional ministry makes conflict inevitable. The key for many spiritual leaders is to avoid responses that aggravate the situation and threaten to unseat the leader's agenda. It is also critical that the leadership corps of any ministry be acquainted with what to expect in terms of conflict so they are not caught off guard. Books and seminars abound to help with this. One key but often overlooked element for leaders is the personal dimension of conflict, understanding why we respond the way we do in those situations. If the responses involve fear or arrogance or feelings of insecurity, it's likely that personal psychological factors are driving it. A good learning discipline here for the leader is to work with a competent coach to debrief the last several conflict situations at home or in a leadership setting to make personal discoveries of your own conflict style and learn to develop a broader repertoire of responses.

## Transition Leadership

While most people understand that change must occur, it's usually not the changes that do them in. It is the transition—the emotional processing of change. Its stages are predictable: first we deny we need to change, then we resist it, then we begin to explore it, and finally we commit to making it. Good leaders know the strategies for dealing with each stage, both in themselves and with the people in their leadership constellation. There are many good print resources available for education in transition leadership. Your local business school might offer a class or seminar in this area. Another source of training would be to interview one or more leaders who have successfully navigated transition in their lives and organizations. Don't overlook health care leaders and educational administrators, particularly at the college level. Because these sectors have undergone so much transition over the past few years, many of their leaders have lots of experiential expertise to share.

## Listening Skills

Most people's listening skills improve when they choose to make it a priority, since listening is largely a matter of focus and intentionality. However, some print resources are available to help you improve this important leadership skill. When people are convinced that we are listening, their responses are likely to be less antagonistic if they are resisting and much more committed if they are in agreement. One way to develop metrics for this area is to track the perceptions of people around you in terms of your own listening. Let them rate you. Spouses and kids go first.

## Celebrating Others and Self

The capacity to celebrate others' achievements is an essential part of changing the culture of an organization, because, as noted earlier, what gets rewarded is what gets done. The efforts to create a scorecard for each shift are opportunities to set up celebrations as you achieve benchmarks. For many spiritual leaders, the capacity to celebrate others and themselves has been dulled by not understanding that most people are motivated by affirmation. Personal psychological issues also some into play, as when a perfectionist leader withholds celebration because an effort isn't perfect. Furthermore, a leader who mistakenly thinks humility prevents a person from being able to celebrate achievement will hold back on those kinds of celebrations. The ability to celebrate is an essential element in building a personal and organizational strengths-based approach. The leader's growth in this area starts with a look at the leader's own assumptions about self and about people and how they grow. This will necessarily involve feedback from people in the leader's constellation, including family, and skilled debriefing with a coach or counselor.

## Missionary Training

Many spiritual leaders have no training in developing missionaries because that has been left to professionals in denominations and parachurch ministries. If we are going to turn members into missionaries, it is essential that this skill be added to the portfolio of leadership capacities. An obvious place to turn for process and content would be to people who currently conduct training for missionary service. Missionary training involves cultural and language studies; the same is true when training local missionaries: we must help them understand the language of our own culture. One place to begin is with generational studies, since the generational cohorts in our society now represent distinct cultures.

## Praying

Jesus invites us to ask for the kingdom. Missional leaders who focus on kingdom-oriented leadership may need to get better at this. Regarding prayer as a way to rehearse needs with God is one way to go at it. Seeing it as a way to tune in to the frequency of what God is saying and doing is another. Kingdom-focused leaders pursue the latter, meaning that prayer is much more dialogical and much more geared to listening than to informing God of things he already knows. Although leaders may need to devote more time to prayer, the evaluation of the content of that time is equally important.

## Resource Management

Just as leaders have to make sure organizational resources are refocused in order to be more intentionally missional, so they need to make sure they take the same approach to their own lives. Since I am suggesting that you think through each leadership development item with the following resources in mind, any listing in these categories would be redundant or even confusing. However, I do want to say a few things about how the leader can apply or recalibrate these resources toward being more missional.

### Prayer

Having a specific prayer agenda that is missionally informed is a change for many leaders. Evaluating your own prayer rhythms and processes should also be a priority for your investigation. What do you pray for, when, and how? You will find your praying content and process shifting along with your move to missional. I recommend recruiting a personal prayer support team and then figuring out how to update these helpers on your personal and leadership needs. When recruiting this team, you may even want to ask people to focus their prayers on specific aspects of your life and ministry instead of covering the waterfront with each one. My own prayer support team as a local congregational leader included three groups of people, some praying for my preaching (if you ever hear me preach, you'll understand the need for this), others for my leadership responsibilities, and a few focused on my personal and family heath.

## Relationships

Missional leadership begins at home. Engaging your family in a missional lifestyle is not only a matter of integrity but also the surest sign to observers that you are serious about this matter. Remember, what people see you doing is what they think is important to you—because it is! Your other categories of relationships, including friends, coworkers, and fellow leaders, will also be affected by your new missional focus. Your friendships might include more people who are not currently Jesus followers. Your coworkers will be beneficiaries of your commitment to people development because you will be interested in their personal growth, not just their job performance. In fact, their personal development will be the centerpiece of your evaluation and coaching. Your ministry organization leaders will find themselves challenged by you as well as instructed and coached by you into their own missional lives. What you model at home and with your staff will set the pattern for their evaluation of their own missional journeys.

## Time

How you spend your time will tell the tale. You might need to conduct a personal time audit to find out where your time is currently going so you will be able to make informed decisions about how to refocus it toward greater missional intentionality. Be ruthless with yourself in this self-management category. You are probably going to have to make some very difficult choices. Your reallocation will likely have repercussions. Take these into account, maybe even taking the people who might be affected into your counsel as you move to make the changes. You might even find yourself doing less, dialing time off and Sabbath back into your life as you figure out that your own personal development requires additional time allocation.

## Money

Pay attention here to both corporate and personal management. Your ministry leadership decisions will certainly affect budgeting, resourcing strategies, and spending priorities. This will probably be true of your personal finances as well. Don't neglect developing some personal metrics to combat Mammon, freeing up ways that your personal stewardship can bless other people. An evaluation of lifestyle choices—how you spend your money, on what—is a crucial part of establishing a developmental path. This will likely involve other people in your family. They will need to be included in this evaluation. Otherwise, you may find your best intentions unintentionally thwarted or even deliberately sabotaged by those closest to you.

## Technology

Make technology work for you; don't work for it. Figure out ways to serve your missional agenda through applied technology, such as e-mail or text-messaged updates for prayer partners. But also look out for ways that technology invades time and saps energy from your leadership. The way you use your cell phone and PDA may place you at risk of greater distraction. Realize that your e-mail may not always have to be opened or even answered. If you figure out that you are a gadget geek or techno junkie, you may have to go on a technology diet.

## Personal Property

How you use your physical resources is part of a missional strategy for life. Your home, office, cars, vacation properties—the things in your life—are all part of the life you will have to manage from a greater missional perspective. For some people, this will involve opening up these resources for use, no longer treating what we have as ours alone. For others, the need will be just the opposite, to define greater boundaries for emotional health to safeguard personal space and family provision. A lot of evaluation in this area will overlap with other resource allocations, such as the time we spend on the things in our lives and how we spend our money.

## Personal Growth

It *is* all about you—at least when it comes to taking responsibility for living the life you want with intentionality. Too many leaders lose life in leadership. This is not God's design and does not reflect spiritual devotion. The truth is that God is more interested in turning you into a person than into anything else! It's the hardest work he does, and it's going to take him all your life to do it.

The missional message is incarnational, meaning it is wrapped up in you. That's why paying close attention to your personal growth is a missional strategy. Personal growth can't be templated. However, I have found some issues and concerns that seem to resonate with most leaders I have worked with as the most critical ones to monitor. I want to identify these for you and make a comment or two on each one. (I give much expanded attention to these and other leadership issues in *Practicing Greatness*.[1]) You will want to make sure you have adequately explored these areas of concern. Don't be overwhelmed at the list. Perhaps you have dealt with most of these issues already. Maybe you just need to check in with some trusted people to make sure you are OK in these areas.

For items you choose to work on, you will more than likely need the help of some other people. Who these people are will vary depending on the subject. In every case, whether it is engaging a gifted counselor who can help you with boundary issues or going to see a financial adviser, see this as an investment in the most important thing you bring to your leadership—you!

## Self-Awareness

Self-awareness is the single most important information that a leader possesses. Without this, you do not know why you do what you do. You may simply be reacting to someone's pulling your chain. Or your leadership may be based on some internal sense of deficit such that you always feel you have something to prove. Maybe you need lots of affirmation to perform well. Having the chance to do something no one else has done might be the motivation that pushes you to risk. You need to know these things about yourself—your motivations, fears, tendencies, and so on. Your effectiveness as a missional leader is greatly enhanced by being self-aware. The following categories are essential to that understanding.

• *Personality strengths and challenges.* Many leaders feel that their personality is something they need to get over. The truth is that our personalities are simply the way we prefer to engage the world. There is nothing wrong with being introverted or wanting to be selectively social, just as there is nothing wrong with preferring to have people around all the time. The key is to know when to dial down or dial up our personalities. But unless we know what our strengths and challenges are, we are unable to exercise disciplined control. We are only reacting.

• *Cognitive style.* The way our brains process information affects everything from mood to personality to decision making. Some of us go into ourselves to figure out what we think through reading and reflection, while others of us don't know what we think until we hear ourselves say it out loud to someone else. Some of us are highly conceptual thinkers, seeing the big picture. Others prefer to work with the information at close range, one piece at a time. Some leaders can make decisions with very little information while others build a case until they reach a point of feeling comfortable with the amount of input they have obtained. Part of the benefit of determining your cognitive style is the realization that everyone doesn't think like you think. When we impose our own style on other people, we can get really frustrated because they don't respond the way we do. This can even lead to a disruption of relationships.

• *Conflict style.* Our conflict styles are usually learned in our family of origin or in our first position with leadership responsibilities, especially if conflict was significant. Some of us grew up in families of screamers; others learned to be punitive; some developed an avoidance to conflict; still others tend to be conflict-allergic. Since every leadership role of significance involves conflict at some point, leaders need to know how they typically respond. Their response can be modified once it is understood.

• *Emotional intelligence.* This is leaders' capacity for knowing how they come across to other people. Leaders who lack emotional intelligence frequently fail to understand others' emotional needs and responses. They consequently falter in their attempts to build significant relationships with their followers.

• *Talent.* Nowhere in Scripture are we told we are going to be held accountable for talent we don't have. However, we are informed that we will be responsible for the stewardship of what we have been given. An honest assessment of talent provides an understanding of your potential and where you should be directing your energies. Talent matters. Your best shot at making your most worthy leadership contribution is for you to get better at what you are already good at. Building a culture of strengths begins with the leader.

• *Passions.* Your passions help define you and can serve as a way of discerning God's plan for your missional interface with the world. Your passions can be determined by what brings you energy or fuels your imagination. Passion tugs at your heartstrings in terms of some improvement you'd like to make or cause you'd like to champion.

• *Hidden addictions and compulsions*. We carry these from our families of origin, typically. I call these hidden because the leader usually is not aware of them, not because the condition itself is hidden. In fact, others are often well aware of the dark sides of leaders. The possible range of problem areas is vast—work, food, sex, and control are a few common ones—contributing to a variety of compulsive behaviors. These issues can rarely be treated by the leader without some kind of professional help and strong emotional support from spouse and close friends.

## Family Development

As you intentionally develop your family relationships with a missional emphasis, some important activities and practices emerge. These become benchmarks for assessing the missional development of your family.

• *Spousal relationship*. The call to serve the world is not a call to neglect the person we've invited to share our journey. Paying attention to this most intimate of relationships always brings a great return on investment. Figuring out together how you want to live missionally as a couple is an important developmental strategy for an enhanced marriage.

• *Children*. Missional living begins with making sure that the family is a blessing place where people development is primary to the culture. Missional leaders as parents make sure their children learn from an early age to be blessings to those around them at school, in the neighborhood, at work, on the athletic field, or in the concert chamber. These parents also intentionally practice life debriefing as a routine part of every day, beginning when their children are young, so that by the teenage years, healthy conversations can be engaged in as issues of growing up become more complex. Missional families serve together, reaping the rewards of being bonded together through these experiences.

## Emotional and Spiritual Health

Leaders also need to pay very close attention to issues of emotional and spiritual health. These are usually interrelated.

• *Spiritual disciplines.* I assume that you practice the usual and classical disciplines of prayer, Bible study, fasting, serving, and giving, because we never outgrow the need for them. But you also need to pay attention to the discipline of observing Sabbath, making sure that you are routinely spending important time breaking the work rhythm. This allows you to accomplish two things. First, Sabbath involves spending time with the Lover of your soul. Second, practicing Sabbath allows you to debrief life with Coach. Leaders who have his perspective plowed into their lives on a regular basis operate with much greater insight and fruitfulness. Spiritual health is also affected by the condition of our relationships across the board, with family, coworkers, and friends. Broken relationships take a huge toll in soul strength. Practicing forgiveness and seeking reconciliation are key to ridding yourself of toxins that poison your spirit.

• *Emotional health.* Items in this category include dealing with difficult emotions (anger in particular), managing depression (a common plague of spiritual leaders), and developing healthy friendships, all of which increase emotional resiliency. Emotional health is also strengthened by developing hobbies and taking work assignments that are consonant with your strengths but that also keep you emotionally energized and engaged. Most of the ministry burnout I have encountered over the years comes from leaders' working in areas where they are weak or lack passion. Our strengths are also our needs. If we don't get to do what we are good at, our soul feels undernourished. Finally, a key challenge to the emotional health of spiritual leaders comes in the form of boundary mismanagement. Enforcing appropriate boundaries is critical for maintaining emotional and psychological health.

## Physical Health

Personal growth includes paying attention to the bodies God gave us so that we are good stewards of these vessels. Raising this issue doesn't mean that missional leaders spend most of their time in the gym or are specimens of physical prowess. In fact, many missional leaders are physically challenged. Again, the issue is stewardship of this resource that either enhances or diminishes the leader's effectiveness.

• *Nutrition.* The idea here is not only to eat smart but to learn which foods might trigger allergic reactions in your body. Learning which combinations and types of foods bring you energy can improve your well-being.

• *Exercise regimen.* There are many benefits to regular exercise. Among them are the benefits to an often-overlooked organ of the body, the brain. Exercise releases chemicals that cleanse the brain as well as stimulate pleasure.

• *Adequate sleep.* We are becoming increasingly aware of the importance of rest. This is true for every body system, including our mental disposition and our heart health. Errors of judgment and loss of emotional restraint as well as heightened anxiety are common maladies associated with inadequate sleep.

• *Appropriate medical checkups and treatment.* Go see the doctor! I can't tell you how many leaders I have encouraged to see physicians for treatment of ailments from the simply annoying all the way up to life-threatening. Part of this is to make sure that you are paying attention to the medications you are taking, with an eye toward potentially dangerous drug interactions.

## Financial Health

Being a spiritually attuned leader doesn't cancel out bad credit. Missional leaders, like everyone else, need to monitor their financial health. I have seen too many spiritual leaders who are constantly distracted by the background noise in their lives of poor financial conditions. It takes its toll in lack of concentration but can take an even more serious toll on the leader's credibility if the problems spill out into the public.

• *Personal and family spending plan.* This is called a budget in some circles. It's not fun for most people to develop, but it is a way of avoiding financial disaster. Indeed, adherence to a budget alleviates a lot of anxiety that can arise when decisions are made without an overall plan. A bunch of items should be a part of the budget, including charitable giving, savings, insurance, retirement, and fun stuff like vacations and movies.

• *Financial plan.* Having a professional help you with a financial plan can get you on an intentional path of preparing for the future. Typical plans will help you make provisions for your own life and also beyond, with some estate planning. Good financial planners will also incorporate items such as consideration of whether you need long-term care insurance and how much, disability insurance, health care decision making and durable power of attorney issues—everything you need to consider to put your financial house in order.

• *Income enhancement.* Too many spiritual leaders suffer from too little income. For some, remedies can be found, especially with a little thought. Part of the character of missional leadership is that it will frequently involve managing a portfolio of income streams that support it, ranging from jobs to personal benefactors and many options and combinations in between. Get in front of this by having a proactive strategy. Take courses, explore job markets, cultivate donors, and clarify your mission so that you and your mission are worth investing in.

## Developing the Scorecard

At this point, you may feel all I've left out is the kitchen sink. But there is a reason that these particular concerns needed to be mentioned. These areas of personal growth are where the rubber meets the road between intention and actual achievement. They can't all be addressed at once, and you will almost surely be giving differing levels of attention to different items. The key is to make sure that over time, these issues are appropriately addressed.

You might want to start with an item or two in each section. Sketch out what it would look like if you enjoyed a sense of achievement in that area. Then think through some specific actions that will get you going in that direction. You probably can't put away all the money for retirement by age thirty-five, but you would want to be actively pursuing a retirement goal by then. You can't lose those twenty pounds next week, but you can in the next three to four months. Break it down; lay it out. Be as specific as you can. Get people who have expertise in these areas to help you. Then be accountable. One leader I know listed his weight each week with his staff until he had it under control. And by all means, make sure some people are cheering for you!

You are not incidental to your leadership! We will not have a sustained missional movement without vibrant missional people, including those who provide leadership. That means that paying attention to your personal growth and development is vital to the cause. The "imitate me" nature of kingdom leaders demands that theirs be a life worth desiring. No one else will hand that life to you. It will take deliberate lifelong effort. The price is high for such intentionality. But I have never met anyone living in the fruit of their intentionality that felt the price was too great.

Andrew ended his e-mail to me on this upbeat note: "I'm loving this new season of life and ministry, and my wife and kids are engaged in this new kingdom adventure." Sounds like the refrain of missional people to me! You can sing this same song if you develop and implement a personal leadership missional scorecard.

# CONCLUSION

I was treated to a window view into the missional renaissance just yesterday over Jones sodas at a booth in Panera Bread. Brad Smith was the one who pulled back the drape. He is the founder of the Souper Bowl of Caring (http://www.souperbowl.org). We had never met before, so he was detailing for me the remarkable story and impact of this charitable venture. Now in its twenty-first year, this movement last year raised $10 million for hunger relief and engaged 250,000 young people in volunteer service in their communities around the nation.

The Souper Bowl of Caring started out as a project in the youth ministry of Spring Valley Presbyterian Church in Columbia, South Carolina, where Brad served as youth pastor at the time. The idea was to capitalize on the biggest sporting event of the year, football's Super Bowl, to provide a service opportunity for teenagers. Kids collected donations to fight local hunger and poverty. Over the next few years, other churches in the area who heard about it quickly adopted it; then churches jumped on board from other regions of the country and other denominations. The Souper Bowl of Caring became a movement, involving over 14,000 groups of volunteers in 2008. Brad eventually left his church job to devote full-time efforts to shepherding its development. Players now include schools as well as churches, adults as well as teenagers, foundations and family charities, NFL team owners, and other social sector organizations. Brad's dream is that Super Bowl weekend will become the biggest weekend of charitable efforts and giving in the country each year.

This is the missional renaissance in full flower. All elements are present. You have a movement that involves cross-domain collaboration for tackling a huge social issue. Not only do the efforts of the participants benefit others, but the participants themselves also grow by fulfilling their own fundamental needs as human beings to serve others. The Souper Bowl of Caring is led by a true kingdom-oriented leader who raises his own support and the money it takes to pay staff and cover program and administrative costs. The goal is not to build an organization (the whole operation is run by a staff of six). The Souper Bowl office doesn't even collect the money it helps people raise. Decisions about where the money goes is left to the people who raise it and who are knowledgeable about local needs.

Community needs are being met. People are being developed. The leadership approach fosters the movement by empowering people and releasing passion and resources. And it all started with an idea from a spiritual leader who had an ache in his heart to alleviate suffering and a determination to help teenagers discover the benefits of serving. All three shifts of the missional movement are right there. If this story didn't exist, I'd have to make it up! Thankfully, it does exist, and the world is better for it.

Little of this development could have been imagined all those years ago when this idea was born. Twenty years ago, churches did their church thing, and hunger was dealt with largely by social and governmental agencies. But the rise of the altruism economy, the widespread desire of people to grow by giving of themselves, and an increased openness to spirituality (the Souper Bowl movement is faith-based)—three formative developments I've identified as giving rise to the missional renaissance—have created a cultural climate just right for sup-porting a movement like this.

This cultural milieu, powered and shaped by these three sig-nificant forces, is changing the spiritual landscape before our very eyes. Some of the manifestations we are likely to see as a result include the following.

• Disinterest in institutional cultural Christianity will accelerate.

• Churches that thrive will become more externally focused in their ministry agenda and more intentional in developing their people. These efforts will be led by people who have a dif-ferent leadership agenda than institutional church issues and concerns. These shifts are the three elements involved in going missional. This book has been written largely to help church people and church leaders who want to go here. The biggest challenge will be to replace the current scorecard to force a change in behavior informed by these shifts.

• An explosion of missional communities (MCs) will occur. These will be groups of believers and nonbelievers who will operate in noninstitutional settings. They will range in size from a handful of participants to a few dozen. Gatherings will take place in homes and restaurants, bookstores and bars, office con-ference rooms and university dorm rooms, hotel meeting areas and downtown Ys, and yes, even churches.

Their community life will center on an intense desire to grow spiritually and to aid the community. Some MCs will be connected to churches; many will not be. Affinities will be com-mon passions and similar life rhythms. Leadership will emerge from within. Biblical teaching will be imported through pod-casts, DVDs, and books.

MCs will order their lives around communion, caring, and celebration. Communion will include eating together as well as sharing the sacraments. Caring will be lavished on each other but also extend to people beyond the MC as part of the group's expression of following Jesus. As a result, more people will become Jesus followers. Celebration will highlight this work of God in the lives of those in the MC as well as rehearse God's revelation in history and in text. MCs will routinely serve together and with others while participants will be cheered to be missional in their own lives as Jesus followers. Networks of these missional communities may be sponsored by large existing churches; others will form in regions along relational lines.

• Increasing numbers of Jesus followers will live out their missional expression in the context of their family and work environments. These will not be "loners" but will go through life with a few close friends. This approach to life serves their sense of community and satisfies their need to belong. Their practice of corporate gathering with the larger body of Christ will be accomplished by attending church services on special occasions. They will join other Jesus followers periodically in projects that pull them together. For the most part, they will focus their missional energies pretty closely on the world they inhabit every day.

• Churches and church leaders who understand the missional impulse will sponsor and celebrate these new expressions of "being church."

• Many leaders of the missional movement will not be clergy. Credentialing for leadership through theological education will yield to credentialing through passion and personal leadership competencies. Leadership potential will be recognized locally and then ratified by judicatories, as opposed to the way clergy credentialing has traditionally been approached (appointment by the judicatory and then ratification by the local congregation).

• Many clergy will be able to transition their current ministry assignments into missional expressions. Again, this book has been written specifically to support this transition by giving these leaders language and actions that will result in different thinking and different behavior.

• Many clergy will not be able to make this transition in their current church roles. Consequently, they will move into the marketplace for employment in pursuit of their call to be missional leaders. Some will discover that their personal identity is tied up in their clergy role. This will precipitate a crisis that will become life-defining. Those who grapple with this issue and come out well will experience great release and freedom to serve.

• The current dominant affiliations based on doctrinal agreement and denominational polity will be replaced by those of common compassion and life orientation. The spiritual agenda will be less issue-oriented and more centered around loving God and loving others as the core attitudes and actions of genuine Jesus followers.

• Spiritual literature will increasingly focus on helping people become more intentional Jesus followers in their natural habitats through home, office, school, and street applications of biblical truth.

• Those who shudder at these developments will likely miss the party. Those who welcome the new work of God will paddle like crazy with all their might to go out and catch the big wave.

Some of you reading this are ripe candidates for leading the missional church movement. You have a passion and a dream. That is a powerful combination when you serve as the King's representative and see his kingdom everywhere. Your impact may be across the street or around the world. You will create new worlds of human possibility and kingdom reality. Others from all sectors of the community will come alongside you to participate in what you see God doing. God will be pleased. People will be better off. Those are the two rewards you seek. It will be impossible to imagine the world as it was before you showed up.

Welcome to the missional renaissance! You have been sent by God. The world is glad you came.

# NOTES

## Chapter One

1. Bill Clinton, *Giving* (New York: Knopf, 2007).
2. David Kinnaman and Gabe Lyons, *Unchristian* (Grand Rapids, Mich.: Baker Books, 2007), p. 226.
3. Pew Forum on Religion and Public Life, U.S. *Religious Landscape Survey* (Washington, D.C.: Pew Forum, 2008), available at http://religions.pewforum.org/

## Chapter Two

1. "Missional Church: From Sending to Being Sent," in Darrell L. Guder, ed., *Missional Church: A Vision for the Sending of the Church in North America* (Grand Rapids, Mich.: Eerdmans, 1998), p. 4.
2. David Bosch, *Transforming Mission: Paradigm Shifts in Theology of Mission* (Maryknoll, N.Y.: Orbis Books, 1991), p. 390.
3. Lois Y. Barrett, Darrell L. Guder, and Walter C. Hobbs, *Treasures in Clay Jars: Patterns in Missional Faithfulness* (Grand Rapids, Mich.: Eerdmans, 2004), p. x.
4. Leslie Newbigin, *The Gospel in a Pluralistic Society* (Grand Rapids, Mich.: Eerdmans, 1989), pp. 128–129.

5.  George R. Hunsberger, "Sizing Up the Shape of the Church," in *Between Gospel and Culture: The Emerging Mission in North America*, ed. George R. Hunsberger and Craig Van Gelder (Grand Rapids, Mich.: Eerdmans, 1996), pp. 333–346.
6.  Newbigin, *Gospel in a Pluralistic Society*, p. 134.
7.  Michael Frost and Alan Hirsch, *The Shaping of Things to Come* (Peabody, Mass.: Hendrickson, 2003), p. 30.

## Chapter Three

1.  Rick Rusaw and Eric Swanson, *The Externally Focused Church* (Loveland, Colo.: Group Publishing, 2004).
2.  Pew Forum, *U.S. Religious Landscape Survey*.
3.  See Neil Cole, *Organic Church: Growing Faith Where Life Happens* (San Francisco: Jossey-Bass, 2005).
4.  Robert Lewis with Rob Wilkins, *The Church of Irresistible Influence* (Grand Rapids, Mich.: Zondervan, 2001).
5.  See Michael Frost, *Exiles: Living Missionally in a Post-Christian Culture* (Peabody, Mass.: Hendrickson, 2007). See also Frost and Hirsch, *Shaping of Things to Come*.
6.  See Joanne Appleton, *Mid Sized Mission: The Use of Mid Size Groups as a Vital Strategic Component of Church Planting*, European Church Planting Network, Concept Paper 1, available at http://leadnet.org/downloads/Mid-Sized%20Mis sional%20Groups.pdf
7.  See Bob Hopkins and Mike Breen, *Clusters: Creative Mid-Sized Missional Communities* (Sheffield, England: Anglican Church Planting Initiatives, 2008).
8.  See "Discipleship: Lifeshapes," 3 Dimension Ministries, http://www.3dministries.com
9.  On the Adullam community, see Hugh Halter and Matt Smay, *The Tangible Kingdom: Creating Incarnational Community* (San Francisco: Jossey-Bass, 2008).

## Chapter Five

1. See Kinnaman and Lyons, *Unchristian.*
2. Greg L. Hawkins and Cally Parkinson, *Reveal: Where Are You?* (Barrington, Ill.: Willow Creek Association, 2007).

## Chapter Seven

1. The year A.D. 30 is widely accepted as the year of Jesus' death, Resurrection, and ascension.
2. See Alan Hirsch, *The Forgotten Ways: Reactivating the Missional Church* (Wheaton, Ill.: Brazos Press, 2006).

## Chapter Eight

1. Reggie McNeal, *Practicing Greatness: Seven Disciplines of Extraordinary Spiritual Leaders* (San Francisco: Jossey-Bass, 2006).

# THE AUTHOR

*Dr. Reggie McNeal* is the missional leadership specialist for Leadership Network of Dallas, Texas. His past experience includes twenty syears in local church leadership, including ten years as a founding pastor of a new church, and over a decade as a denominational executive focused on leadership development. He has lectured or served as adjunct faculty for multiple seminaries, including Southwestern Baptist (Fort Worth, Texas), Golden Gate Baptist (San Francisco), Fuller Theological (Pasadena, California), Trinity Divinity School (Deerfield, Illinois), and Columbia International (Columbia, South Carolina). In addition, McNeal has been a consultant to local church, denomination, and parachurch leadership teams, as well as seminar developer and presenter for thousands of church leaders across North America. He has served as a resource for the United States Army Chief of Chaplains Office, Air Force chaplains, and the Air Force Education and Training Command. McNeal's work also extends to the business sector, including the Gallup Organization. He has contributed to numerous denominational publications and church leadership journals. His books include *Revolution in Leadership: Training Apostles for Tomorrow's Church* (Abingdon Press, 1998), *A Work of Heart: Understanding How God Shapes Spiritual Leaders* (Jossey-Bass, 2000), *The Present Future: Six Tough Questions for the Church* (Jossey-Bass, 2003),

*Practicing Greatness: Seven Disciplines of Extraordinary Spiritual Leaders* (Jossey-Bass, 2006), and *Get a Life! It Is All About You* (Broadman & Holman, 2007). McNeal's education includes a bachelor of arts degree from the University of South Carolina and master of divinity and doctor of philosophy degrees from Southwestern Baptist Theological Seminary. McNeal and his wife, Cathy, have two daughters, Jessica and Susanna, and make their home in Columbia, South Carolina.

# INDEX

## A

Abraham, 27–28, 36, 37, 46–47
Acts, Book of, 36
A.D. 30 leadership, 131–136
Adam, 35
Addictions, 171
Adullam community, 64
Affiliation, religious, 13, 56
Age groups, 108–109
Altruism economy, emergence of, 4–6
*American Idol* (television series), 5
Apostles, role of, 142
Apostolic leadership, 131–133
Assyrians, 28
Attractional church, 49–56, 58

## B

Babylon, 29
Beautiful Day movement, 151
Behavioral approach, and helping
    people, 103–104
Bible, and missional perspective, 26–34
Bible teaching, 56–57
Bivocational model, of income sources,
    153
Blackaby, H., 23
Blessing strategy, 46–49, 57
Blogs, 86
Bosch, D., 21
Breen, M., 63
Brilliant, L., 4
Budget, 174

## C

Calendar. *See* Time
Call, and missional ministry, 154–156
Capital stewardship drive, 83
Cathedrals, in Europe, 141–143
Celebration, of others and self, 163–164
Cell-phone technology, 86
Chaplains, in military, 136–137
Charitable giving, 4–6
Children, and leadership, 171–172
*Chronicles of Narnia* (Lewis), 155–156
Church: nature of, 19–20, 22–24, 49–53,
    57–58; role of, 46–49
Church-based leadership, shift from,
    14–15, 129–156
Church-centric perspective, 42–45
Church growth movement, 92
*The Church of Irresistible Influence*
    (Lewis), 62
Clergy: and income sources, 152–154,
    174; role of, 134–143, 150–152;
    training of, 11. *See also* Leadership
Clinton, B., 4
Clusters, as missional communities,
    63–64
Coaching, as leadership skill, 161
Cognitive style, and leadership, 169–170
Cole, N., 63–64
Columbia, South Carolina, 177–178
Community leaders, and prayer, 72
Community ministries capital drive, 83
Community, prayer for, 72–73
Community prayer meetings, 73

Community service, and corporations, 4–5
Compartmentalization, 106–108
Compulsions, and leadership, 171
Conflict management, as leadership skill, 162
Conflict style, and leadership, 170
Congregations, shift from, 62–65
Connect-and-deploy modality, of missional church, 59–60
Constantine, 13–14, 62, 131
Conversations, case study in, 122–127
Coordinated prayer, 74
1 Corinthians 4:16, 147
Curriculum-centered approach, 104–105
Customization, 95–97

**D**

Debriefing, concept of, 101–103
Demonstration, of love and service, 56–57
Denver, Colorado, 64
Deploy-and-debrief method, of leadership training, 143–146
Development offices, 84
Didactic approach, and helping people, 103–104
Director, clergy as, 139–141
Donations, 4–6
Drucker, P., 78

**E**

Education, nature of, 8–9
Egypt, 29
Emotional health, and leadership, 172–173
Emotional intelligence, and leadership, 170
Employment, and clergy, 152–154, 174
Empowerment, and information, 8–9
Ephesians 4:13, 31
Evangelicals, 32
Evangelism, 43, 47
Exercise regimen, 173
Exodus 19:5-6, 29
Exodus saga, 28
External ministry focus, 6–7, 41–87
The Externally Focused Church (Rusaw and Swanson), 41
Extreme Makeover: Home Edition (television series), 5

**F**

Facilities, and resource reallocation, 79–82, 120–121
Faith-based government initiatives, 84
Families, role of, 108–109
Family development, and leadership, 171–172
FAQs (frequently asked questions), 147–156
Fellowship Bible Church, 62
50 First Dates (film), 34
Finances, and resource reallocation, 82–85, 119–120, 167
Financial health, 174
Financial planning seminars, 84
Focus, of ministry, 6–7, 41–87
FreeRice.com, 5
Frequently asked questions (FAQs), 147–156
Frost, M., 23–24, 63
"Full-service" church, 43

**G**

Gaddini, G., 123–127
Garden of Eden, 35
Genesis 12, 27–28, 46–47
Gentiles, 36
Giving (Clinton), 4
"Giving It Away" (edition of New York Times Magazine), 4
God saga, and human drama, 34–38
Grants, 83–84
Great Commission, 34
Groundhog Day (film), 34
Guder, D., 21

**H**

Health issues, 172–173
Hirsch, A., 23–24, 145
Historian, clergy as, 141–143
Hospitality staff in restaurants, and prayer, 73
Human drama, and God saga, 34–38
Hunsberger, G., 22

**I**

The Incarnation, 22, 34, 35
Incarnational church, 49–58, 60–62. See also Missional church
Income sources, for clergy, 152–154, 174

Information, and empowerment, 8–9
Institutional church, shift from, 57–58
Institutional representative, clergy as, 136–139
Integration, shift to, 106–109
Intergenerational environments, 108–109
Internal ministry focus, shift from, 6–7, 41–66
Internet, 74, 86–87
Iraq war, 136

**J**

Jesus: childhood of, 29–31; and deploy-and-debrief method, 144; as high priest, 28; and Incarnation, 35; and Pharisees, 37
Jethro, 28
John 3:16, 30
John 4, 158–159
John 10:10b, 31
John 20:21b, 33
Jonah, 28
Journalist, clergy as, 141–143

**K**

Kingdom advance, 37
Kingdom-based leadership, 14–15, 129–156, 157–175
Kingdom-focused perspective, 42–45
Kinnaman, D., 6

**L**

Leadership: in kingdom-based church, 129–156, 157–175; and people development, 118; and resource reallocation, 75–76; shift in, 14–15; and type of church, 50–51
Lewis, C. S., 155–156
Lewis, R., 62
Life-centered approach, 104–105
Life coaching, and clergy, 151
Lifelong learning, 8
Lifeshapes Triangle, 63
Listening skills, and leadership, 163
Little Rock, Arkansas, 62
Lost people, praying for, 73–74
Love, and truth, 32
Lyons, G., 6

**M**

Matthew 5:13-15, 33
Matthew 22:37-40, 30
Maturation, 100
McNeal, R., 168
Medical checkups, need for, 173
Melchizedek, 28
Member culture, and attractional church, 54–56
Microeconomic developments, 84–85
Microskill development, and leadership, 161–165
Midsize groups, as missional communities, 63–64
Ministry constituency, 116–118
Ministry, focus of, 6–7, 41–87
Mission, concept of, 20–24
Missional church: and connect-and-deploy modality, 59–60; nature of, xii–xiv, 23–26; as organic, 57–58; and shift to missional communities, 62–65; and shift to missional mode, 38–39; and worship, 60–62
Missional strategists, clergy as, 151
Missionary culture, 54–56. See also External ministry focus
Missionary training, and leadership, 164
Modernity, failures of, 12
Money. See Finances
Moses, 28, 36

**N**

*New York Times Magazine*, 4
Newbigin, L., 23
Nineveh, 28
Nonprofit organizations, 84
Nutrition, 173

**O**

*Oprah's Big Give* (television series), 4
Organic church, shift to, 57–58
Organizational transitional skills, 154
Orthodoxy, maintenance of, 150

**P**

Paradigm issues, and leadership, 158–161
Participation, in program-driven church, 100
Partnerships, 83, 84
Passions, and leadership, 170

Patronage sponsorship, 153
Paul the apostle, 31–32, 36, 132–133
Peninsula Covenant Church, 123–127
Pentecost, 36
People, and resource reallocation, 74–77, 115–118
People development, 10–12, 89–127
People of God, meaning of, 33, 37
Personal growth, 7–9, 116, 168–174
Personal leadership, 146–147
Personal property, and resource reallocation, 167–168
Personality, and leadership, 169–171
1 Peter 2:9, 29
1 Peter 3:15b, 32–33
Peter the apostle, 132–133
Pew Forum on Religion and Public Life, 13, 56
Physical health issues, 173
Positional authority, 146–147
*Practicing Greatness: Seven Disciplines of Extraordinary Spiritual Leaders* (McNeal), 168
Prayer, and resource reallocation, 69–74, 114–115, 165
Prayer request feedback, 74
Pre-Fall era, 35
Preaching, 56–57
*The Present Future: Six Tough Questions for the Church* (McNeal), xiii
*Prince Caspian* (film), 155–156
Proclamation, shift from, 56–57
Producer, clergy as, 139–141
Program development, shift from, 10–12, 89–110
Program-driven church, 23, 91–110, 112–113
Property taxes, 85
Prophets, role of, 142
Public officials, and prayer, 72
*Purpose-Driven Life* (Warren), 7–8

R

Reach-and-assimilate modality, of traditional church, 59–60
Real Talk, 123–127
Redemptive mission, of God, 35
Redwood City, California, 123–127
The Reformation, xi, 22–23
Relationships: in family, 171–172; need for, 110; and resource reallocation, 166

Religious Landscape Survey, 13
The Renaissance, xvi, 3
Resource management, 116
Resources, reallocation of, 68–87, 113–122, 165–168
Restaurant hospitality staff, and prayer, 73
*Reveal: Where Are You?* (Hawkins and Parkinson), 93–94
Rusaw, R., 41

S

Sacred-versus-secular duality, 107
Saint Thomas Crookes, 63
Samaritans, 29, 31, 36
San Jose, California, 151
Scorecard: in attractional church, 50–52; for external focus, 67–87; for helping people grow, 111–127; for incarnational church, 52; and kingdom-based leadership, 157–175; nature of, 16; need for, 37–38
Scripting, of spiritual journey, 97–100
Secular-versus-sacred duality, 107
Segregation, by age, 108–109
Self-awareness, 116, 169–171
"Sentness", concept of, 21, 34
Service, nature of, 60–62, 105–106
Seybert, J., 126
Shaping, of spiritual journey, 97–100
Sheffield, England, 63
"Sizing Up the Shape of the Church" (Hunsberger), 22
Skill development, 116
Sleep, need for, 173
Smith, B., 177–178
Social gospel, 32
Souper Bowl of Caring, 177–178
Spending plan, 174
Spirituality: quest for, 12–14; shaping of, 97–100; and spiritual health, 172–173
Spousal relationships, and leadership, 171
Spring Valley Presbyterian Church, 177–178
Standardization, 95–97
Storytelling, as leadership skill, 161–162
Swanson, E., 41

**T**

Talbert, J., 151
Talent, and leadership, 170
Teaching function, of clergy, 101–103, 150–151
Technology, and resource reallocation, 85–87, 121–122, 167
Text-messaging, 86
Theology, 20–24, 150
Time, and resource reallocation, 78–79, 119, 166
Traditional church, 57–62, 148–149
Train-and-deploy method, of leadership training, 143–146
Training: methods of, 143–146; for missional community leaders, 151–152; and missionaries, 164
Transition leadership, 162–163
Truth, and love, 32

**U**

*Unchristian* (Kinnaman and Lyons), 6
UP-IN-OUT (Lifeshapes Triangle), 63

**V**

Vacation Bible school (VBS), 138–139
Venture capital funds, 85
Viral agent, clergy as, 136–139

**W**

Warren, R., 7–8
Web site, 86–87
Web site prayer, 74
Willow Creek Association, 93–94
Woman at the well story, in John 4, 158–159
Worship, nature of, 60–62

### The Present Future
*Six Tough Questions for the Church*

## REGGIE MCNEAL

AVAILABLE IN PAPERBACK MARCH 2009!
Hardcover | ISBN: 978-0-7879-6568-6
Paperback | ISBN: 978-0-470-45315-5

*"This is the most courageous book I have ever read on church life. McNeal nails the problem on the head. Be prepared to be turned upside down and shaken loose of all your old notions of what church is and should be in today's world."*
— **George Cladis**, senior pastor, Westminster Presbyterian Church, Oklahoma City, Oklahoma and author, *Leading the Team-Based Church*

In *The Present Future*, author, consultant, and church leadership developer Reggie McNeal debunks old assumptions about church leadership and provides an overall strategy to help church leaders move forward in an entirely different and much more effective way.

In this provocative book, McNeal identifies the six most important realities that church leaders must address including: recapturing the spirit of Christianity and replacing "church growth" with a wider vision of kingdom growth; developing disciples instead of church members; fostering the rise of a new apostolic leadership; focusing on spiritual formation rather than church programs; and shifting from prediction and planning to preparation for the challenges of an uncertain world. McNeal contends that by changing the questions church leaders ask themselves about their congregations and their plans, they can frame the core issues and approach the future with new eyes, new purpose, and new ideas.

Written for congregational leaders, pastors, and staff leaders, *The Present Future* captures the urgency of a future that is literally now upon us, in a thoughtful, vigorous way. It is filled with examples of leaders and churches who are emerging into a new identity and purpose, and rediscovering the focus of their mission within new spiritual dimensions.

### The Present Future
### DVD Collection
*Six Tough Questions for the*
*Church, Set*

### REGGIE MCNEAL

ISBN: 978-0-7879-8673-5

*"Reggie McNeal throws a lifeline to church leaders who are struggling with consumer-oriented congregations wanting church for themselves. The Present Future will recharge your passion."*

—**Rev. Robert R. Cushman**, senior pastor, Princeton Alliance Church, Plainsboro, NJ

Despite the many good things we can point to, the many faithful folks who are doing their best, all is not well with the Christian church in America. What's missing, as Reggie McNeal points out in *The Present Future: Six Tough Questions for the Church*, is the gritty realization that the way we are doing church is just plain wrong. And worse than wrong, it jeopardizes the church's mission. In *The Present Future*, Reggie McNeal reframes the issues facing the church, replacing wrong key questions with tough questions that must be asked.

Filmed live before a studio audience, best-selling author Reggie McNeal teaches participants how to recognize the six most important new realities that church leaders must face if they are to move beyond "churchianity" to a more authentic and missional Christian faith. By changing the questions church leaders ask themselves about their congregations and their mission, they can reshape the Christian movement in North America.

The package includes:

- 1 Leader's Guide
- 1 Participant's Guide
- 4 DVDs

Additional Participant's Guides may also be purchased separately,
ISBN: 978-0-7879-9170-8

# A Work of Heart
*Understanding How God Shapes Spiritual Leaders*

## REGGIE MCNEAL

Hardcover | ISBN: 978-0-7879-4288-5

*"It is not just the skills of ministry that are important. The heart-sculpting work of God creates quality ministries.* A Work of Heart *explains how God is shaping each of us for future service."*

—Bob Buford, founding chairman, Leadership Network

No religious leader can thrive without having heart for the job. But in these times of unpredictability–caught up in trying to help others maintain their hearts–few complete their ministries without sometimes neglecting their own spiritual needs.

Reggie McNeal proposes that effective spiritual leaders must become experts in matters of the heart—particularly their own—and leads readers on an excursion into the heart-shaping drama of four major Biblical leaders: Moses, David, Jesus, and Paul.

Using illustrative stories of contemporary church leaders who opened their hearts to God's guidance, McNeal shows how God is still using these same influences to shape the hearts of religious leaders today.

Spiritual leaders must become experts in matters of the heart. They must learn to discern God at work in their own lives, shaping their hearts to embrace the particular ministries to which they are called. *A Work of Heart* shows how God prepares leaders today just as he did in biblical times and helps leaders develop the critical self-understanding they need to fulfill their life assignments from God.

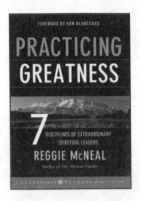

### Practicing Greatness
*7 Disciplines of Extraordinary Spiritual Leaders*

REGGIE MCNEAL

Foreword by Ken Blanchard

Hardcover | ISBN: 978-0-7879-7753-5

*"The depth and breadth of wisdom in this book is just short of unbelievable. Good leaders aspiring to be great leaders will do well to read this book and allow it to probe and shape their lives."*

—Bill Easum, Easum, Bandy & Associates

### How do good spiritual leaders become great leaders?

Based on his experience coaching and mentoring thousands of Christian leaders across a broad spectrum of ministry settings, bestselling leadership expert and consultant Reggie McNeal helps spiritual leaders understand that they will self-select into or out of greatness.

In this important book, McNeal shows how great spiritual leaders are committed consciously and intentionally to seven spiritual disciplines, habits of heart and mind that shape both their character and competence: self-awareness, self-management, a lifelong commitment to self-development through personal growth and learning, a sense of mission, learning to make great decisions, the commitment to live in community, and the intentional practice of solitude and contemplation.

*Practicing Greatness* goes beyond mere clichés and inspirational thoughts to be a hard-hitting resource for leaders who aspire to go from being just good enough to being a great leader who blesses others.

### Reverse Mentoring
*How Young Leaders Can Transform the Church and
Why We Should Let Them*

### EARL CREPS

Hardcover | ISBN: 978-0-470-18898-9

*"The world has ended about four times. New technologies and processes for handling information make the old world obsolete, quickly. When this happens an unusual dynamic asserts itself. Younglings mentor the elders into the way of the new world. The richness of life sharing that is established in reverse mentoring is a largely unexplored, but promising green edge to the Christian movement. Let Earl Creps show you how to get in on this development."*
—Reggie McNeal, author, *Missional Renaissance* and *The Present Future*

In this groundbreaking book, Earl Creps addresses how older ministry leaders can learn from younger peers who are in closer touch with today's culture, technology, and social climate. He reveals the practical benefits of reverse mentoring and offers down-to-earth steps for implementing it at both the personal and the organizational level.

*Reverse Mentoring* offers a guide for leaders who want to experience personal formation by exercising the kind of humility that invites a younger person to become a tutor. Earl Creps details specific benefits of reverse mentoring in areas such as evangelism, communication, and leadership, clearly showing how to develop healthy reverse mentoring relationships that will garner positive results.

*Reverse Mentoring* is a model for church leaders who understand the importance of learning from younger people to prevent functional obsolescence and to transform their leadership and mission.

**EARL CREPS** has been a pastor, ministries consultant, and university professor. Along the way, Creps earned a Ph.D. in communication at Northwestern University and a doctor of ministry degree in leadership at AGTS. He is the author of *Off-Road Disciplines* from Jossey-Bass.

### Organic Church
*Growing Faith Where Life Happens*

## NEIL COLE

Hardcover | ISBN: 978-0-7879-8129-7

*"I heartily recommend this book. It is packed with deep insights; you will find no fluff in it. Among the books on church planting, it offers a rare combination of attributes: it is biblical and well written, its model has proven effective, and it is authored by a practitioner rather than an observer or an ivory-tower theoretician."*

—Curtis Sergeant, director of church planting, Saddleback Church

Leaders and laypeople everywhere are realizing that they need new and more powerful ways to help them spread God's Word. According to international church starter and pastor Neil Cole, if we want to connect with young people and those who are not coming to church, we must go where people congregate.

Cole shows readers how to plant the seeds of the Kingdom of God in the places where life happens and where culture is formed—restaurants, bars, coffeehouses, parks, locker rooms, and neighborhoods. *Organic Church* offers a hands-on guide for demystifying this new model of church and shows the practical aspects of implementing it.

You can find more resources on organic church planting at
www.cmaresources.org

**NEIL COLE** is a church starter and pastor, and founder and executive director of Church Multiplication Associates, which has helped start over seven hundred churches in thirty-two states and twenty-three nations in six years. He is an international speaker and the author of *Cultivating a Life for God*.

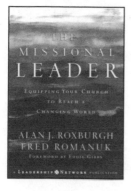

# The Missional Leader
*Equipping Your Church to Reach a Changing World*

## ALAN ROXBURGH AND FRED ROMANUK

Foreword by Eddie Gibbs

Hardcover | ISBN: 978-0-7879-8325-3

*"Discontinuous change wreaks havoc among congregations and pastors who aren't familiar with the new terrain. When it comes to navigating this new land, Roxburgh and Romanuk have my ear and gratitude. Effective, dependable, useful . . . their wisdom is helping retool our congregation for daring and robust witness. And among my students—who feel change deep in their bones, both its threats and opportunities—this book is a vital companion as they begin their ministries."*

—Chris William Erdman, senior pastor, University Presbyterian Church;
adjunct faculty, MB Biblical Seminary Biblical Seminary

In *The Missional Leader*, consultants Alan Roxburgh and Fred Romanuk give church and denominational leaders, pastors, and clergy a clear model for leading the change necessary to create and foster a missional church focused outward to spread the message of the Gospel into the surrounding community.

*The Missional Leader* emphasizes principles rather than institutional forms, shows readers how to move away from "church as usual," and demonstrates what capacities, environments, and mindsets are required to lead a missional church.

**ALAN J. ROXBURGH** is a pastor, teacher, writer, and consultant with more than thirty years experience in church leadership, consulting, and seminary education. He works with the Allelon Missional Leadership Network in the formation of leaders for the missional church.

**FRED ROMANUK** is an organizational psychologist who has led strategic planning initiatives for many large organizations in Canada and the United States. He has also worked with senior executives in assessing and developing the capabilities of people in leadership roles.

## Church Unique

*How Missional Leaders Cast Vision, Capture Culture, and Create Movement*

## WILL MANCINI

Hardcover | ISBN: 978-0-7879-9679-3

*"There is a screaming need today for leaders who will rise above quick fixes and generic approaches. Now, Will Mancini has brought an indispensable book to the church leader's toolbox, providing a thoughtful and creative process that will galvanize your team to unleash God's vision for your church."*

—Howard Hendricks, chairman, Center for Christian Leadership;
distinguished professor, Dallas Theological Seminary

In *Church Unique*, church consultant Will Mancini offers an approach for rethinking what it means to lead with clarity as a visionary. Mancini explains that each church has a culture that reflects its particular values, thoughts, attitudes, and actions, and shows how church leaders can unlock their church's individual DNA and unleash their congregation's one-of-a-kind potential.

Mancini explores the pitfalls churches often fall into in their attempt to grow and explores a new model for vision casting and church growth that has been tested with leaders in all kinds of congregations, including mainline, evangelical, small, and large. The practices and ideas outlined in *Church Unique* will help leaders develop missional teams, articulate unique strategies, unpack the baggage of institutionalism, and live fully into their vision.

Whether leading a megachurch or church plant, a multisite or mainline, a ministry or parachurch, *Church Unique* will provide inspiration as a practical guide for leading into the future. There is a better way.

**WILL MANCINI,** a former pastor, is the founder of Auxano, a national consulting group that works with traditional and emerging churches and ministries of all types around the country. Their mission is to navigate leaders through growth challenges with vision clarity (www.auxano.com).

# The Tangible Kingdom
### Creating Incarnational Community

## HUGH HALTER AND MATT SMAY

Hardcover | ISBN: 978-0-470-18897-2

*"Among increasing numbers of faithful, conservative, Bible-believing Christians, an important shift is beginning to occur. These aren't wild-eyed radicals; they're solid, established church leaders and members who are asking new questions because deep within they discern that something is wrong with the status quo. Hugh and Matt have been through this shift, and offer wise counsel for a way forward."*
—Brian McLaren, author, *A New Kind of Christian* Trilogy and *Everything Must Change*

Written for those who are trying to nurture authentic faith communities and for those who have struggled to retain their faith, *The Tangible Kingdom* offers theological answers and real-life stories that demonstrate how the best ancient church practices can re-emerge in today's culture, through any church of any size.

*The Tangible Kingdom* outlines an innovative model for creating thriving grass-roots faith communities, offering new hope for church leaders, pastors, church planters, and churchgoers who are looking for practical new ways to re-orient their lives to fit God's mission today.

**HUGH HALTER** is a specialist with Church Resource Ministries and the national director of Missio, a global network of missional leaders and church planters. He is also lead architect of Adullam, a congregational network of incarnational communities in Denver, Colorado (www.adullamdenver.com).

**MATT SMAY** co-directs both Missio and Adullam and specializes in helping existing congregations move toward mission. Halter and Smay direct the MCAP "missional church apprenticeship practicum," an international training network for incarnational church planters, pastors, and emerging leaders (www.missio.us).